You Car

Reginald Frary   n
Richmond, Sur   d
draws on his lifetime's experience in his stories of musical mayhem that have entertained countless readers for
almost as long.

This is his fifth volume to be published by the Canterbury Press, and follows the deservedly popular *We Sang it
Our Way, It'll Be All Wrong on the Night, What a Performance* and *Hearts to Heaven and Tempers Raise*.

Also by Reginald Frary and available from the Canterbury Press

We Sang It Our Way
It'll Be All Wrong on the Night
What a Performance
Hearts to Heaven and Tempers Raise

You Can't Keep a Good Tune Down

… no matter how hard the choir tries

Reginald Frary

CANTERBURY PRESS

Norwich

© Reg Frary 2011

First published in 2011 by the Canterbury Press Norwich
Editorial office
13-17 Long Lane,
London, EC1A 9PN, UK

Canterbury Press is an imprint of Hymns Ancient and
Modern Ltd (a registered charity)
13a Hellesdon Park Road, Norwich,
Norfolk, NR6 5DR, UK

www.scm-canterburypress.co.uk

British Library Cataloguing in Publication data

A catalogue record for this book is available from the
British Library

978 1 84825 084 0

Printed and bound in the UK by
CPI UK Reading RG1 8EX

Contents

Preface

There is a superb musical performance that, for me, never fails to bring something of the celestial into the atmosphere of even the most ordinary day. The pure, high sound of a great Welsh male voice choir singing a hymn to a surging Welsh tune by a Welsh composer is a truly thrilling experience.

There are, of course, many other superb church choirs whose singing can also evoke something of the celestial – although, occasionally, one or two members of a congregation may wish that their choir wasn't quite so superb, so that they could sometimes join in the singing of a favourite hymn without fearing that their untrained voices would upset the choir's perfect balance.

Then there are other choirs who definitely don't evoke anything celestial at all. These are those singers, often brought together and presided over by a long-serving, fiercely traditionalist organist, who are constantly and determinedly roaring through nineteenth-century warlike hymns with flamboyant, gung-ho tunes, all about mighty armies of the righteous slaying hordes of the unrighteous, while the vicar, a devotee of loving togetherness praise songs, heroically endures the barbaric bawling at every church service and dutifully thanks the choir for their wonderful enthusiasm.

The choir of the local church may not always be able – even if they try – to satisfy the musical tastes of both clergy and congregation, but in the words of a veteran chorister friend of mine, 'There are many congregational members who know that after all's said and done – and sung – it's often that bolshie crowd up there in the choir stalls who set the pace and keep the whole show on the road.'

Long, long may our church choirs do that!

Reg Frary

1

You Can't Keep a Good Tune Down

All I remembered about Archie before we recently met by chance in London, after the lapse of half a lifetime, was that, as a boy, he had been thrown out of our church choir for, among other heinous sins, drawing uncomplimentary likenesses of the vicar's wife all over the front pages of his *English Hymnal*.

As we reminisced over a meal in a bijou restaurant, where we had taken refuge from a sudden swirling summer downpour, I was intrigued to learn that, like me, Archie was still an active church chorister but that, unlike me, he had progressed to principal tenor and assistant organist and choirmaster at what sounded like a flourishing, traditional small town church in East Anglia. 'I'm retired from business now of course,' he told me. 'The kids have gone off and my wife and I are enjoying ourselves, much involved in the church choir and currently keeping the new vicar from interfering too much in the music with his latest pop praise songs and nightmare ideas for jazzing up the psalms.'

Archie spoke seriously. 'Mind you, our new vicar is a really nice man. The word "nice" is an overworked, often inappropriately used word, but applied to the vicar it is spot-on correct. Everyone in the congregation agrees that he's a really nice man – even the choir doesn't disagree entirely. The trouble for us though is that, although he's a really nice man, he hasn't got a very nice voice – a singing voice, that is. In fact, he can't sing at all. He's got no idea that he can't sing and cheerfully joins in with whatever the choir are singing with a sort of urgent foghorn bellow that we have to make Herculean efforts to overcome so that the congregation can recognize the tune we are supposed to be singing.' Archie looked slightly relieved. 'Fortunately, the vicar doesn't attend choir practice so that *does* keep our choirmaster from becoming too dangerously disturbed and using unacceptable words and expressions in church.'

Archie and I suddenly became aware that the bijou restaurant had now flooded with sunlight as the downpour had swirled away. Simultaneously, we consulted our watches and couldn't believe we'd been sitting talking for so long and, simultaneously, we both realized that we each had just ten minutes to catch our respective trains from our respective stations, so we vowed to keep in touch and ran in opposite directions . . .

We *did* keep in touch and, on a Saturday morning, some weeks after our first encounter since choirboy days, I was on a train travelling towards Archie's country town where I was to spend a few days with him and his wife catching up on how the world had treated us and how we had treated the world during the past forty years.

At the station before my destination there was a sudden huge scuffling hubbub and a crowd of (I imagined) ten-year-olds, all carrying church choir robes, scurried down the rather full carriage, scattering into single available seats. (I was to learn later that they were in fact from Archie's choir, returning from the local music festival.) A rosy faced, rotund lad tripped over his trailing cassock and fell into the seat next to mine. He had a wonderful comical smile. 'Sorry,' he spluttered breathlessly. 'It's this 'ere cassock tangling my feet and our choirgirls all shoving everybody out of the way for seats.' His eyes widened. 'They do that in church in our choir stalls as well y'know. They're *used* to shoving people out of the way – they get together to grab the seats they want. And there's more of them than boys. Well, we've only got three boys now – they call us the last of the Mohicans, although my name is Alfie actually.' He bundled up his cassock into a shaggy ball and gripped it under his chin. 'The vicar says it's all right for the girls to be like they are because it's high time ladies must be seen and heard much more in churches – like being vicars and things, and in any case, he says gentlemen should always give up their seats to ladies.' The comical expression was tinged with indignation. 'Well, I mean ter say, that's all right, giving up your seat to girls, but not when they shove you out of the way before you can even find a seat to *give* them! My friend Ron reckons that the lot we've got in our choir are *not* ladies anyway.' The cassock was threatening to impair Alfie's speech and when it slipped from under his chin I hung it on a convenient hook kindly provided by the railway company. 'That's nice,' he observed appreciatively. 'We have sort of big bent nails to hang our things on in the cassock cupboard in the vestry.

'Our solo girl, she's spoilt. She's got a chrome hanger and a pink plastic cover with horses' heads on it. She *complains* y'see. She's always nagging on and they do things for her because she looks nice and sings "Oh, for the wings of a dove" at weddings and when someone in the congregation has a very old birthday. 'Cause, she *is very good* – brings tears to people's eyes, she does. Not one of us three boys could do that – well, our choirmaster, Mr Grinder – that's not his real name, he's called that because he plays the organ – he says us boys bring tears to *his* eyes at every choir practice, but that's because we keep on singing flat after he's told us not to. We seem to upset him and he calls us utter morons.' Alfie paused to take a hurried, much needed, breath. 'He's a nice man, though. When he started out as a choirmaster there were only boys in our choir – before all these girls came, shoving people about. He's not like the vicar, he treats the girls and us just the same at choir practice. He shouts and says he wonders why he even troubles to try and drum music into our stupid thick heads every Friday night. We all like him though; he's ever so proud of us, really. Every time we win at the music festival – that's where we've been this morning – he's ever so cheerful and takes us all out for a celebration cream tea. And we do always win because there's only us and Holy Trinity choir in the choral class and *they* never win because, Mr Grinder says, they lack the spirit of dedication.' He looked a little puzzled. 'I don't know about that – I think it's because they've got a choirboy who's tone deaf and sings very loudly and no one stops him because his father keeps on giving lots of money for their outings and parties.' He halted, a little breathless again, and the wonderful comical smile was still there. Then, as the train pulled into the station, he grabbed his cassock from the hook, shook hands with me and joined the other two boys leaving the carriage. A

4

bevy of charming little choirgirls, all chattering excitedly, erupted on to the platform and swept aside the last of the Mohicans.

Archie met me on the platform accompanied by his gorgeous Boxer dog, Goss, who I had been warned to greet first because he's very big and prone to knocking people down who don't return his rumbustious greetings immediately. I duly admired him and eventually got round to saying hello to Archie, who was delighted that I'd fully acknowledged Goss. 'Am I right', I speculated, 'that he is named after a favourite composer?' Archie was even more delighted. 'You are a man after my own heart.' He beamed. 'Yes, who else? Sir John Goss, of course – organist of St Paul's Cathedral for years during the nineteenth century – knew Attwood; Stainer was one of his choirboys. Composed great anthems like "The Wilderness", and great hymn tunes like the one for "Praise, my soul, the King of heaven".'

We stood there admiring Goss for a few moments longer, and then Archie suddenly exclaimed urgently, 'And talking of "Praise my soul", we're singing it at three o'clock today. There's been an awful last-minute muck-up over the date of a wedding we had down for next Saturday – something to do with the bride's mother getting the date of her hair-do confused with the actual wedding date. Anyway, it's today and our organist and half the choir can't make it at such short notice so I'm on the organ and you can help me out with the singing. It's all the usual stuff except that *she* wants to come up the aisle to the "Colonel Bogey" march (her dad conducts the local brass band) and *he* wants them to go out to something from "The Twilight of the Gods". It makes you think, doesn't it?!'

Following a quick but absolutely delicious lunch provided by Archie's wonderfully cheerful wife, he and I and Goss were in the choir vestry well before three o'clock, and I was able to meet members of the choir while Archie disappeared into the organ loft to practise 'Colonel Bogey'. There were four men standing in a tight group, three of whom were in a heated argument about football while the fourth kept on announcing that he couldn't understand how normal people could get so het up about a lot of men kicking a ball about. They ceased for a moment to say 'hello' to me and 'where are you from?', and returned with increased vigour to the football theme before I could tell them, and I found myself confronted by two large important-looking ladies whose inadequate choir gowns only partially veiled impressive riding gear. They looked me up and down and nodded dismissively. In a noisy corner romped the junior soprano girls, those who my Mohican averred were always shoving people about. And sitting together on the vestry piano in a show of solidarity were the last of the Mohicans. Alfie recognized me with great surprise. 'Are you a choirman then? We're lucky to have got you here today – half of us are not here and we shan't be strong enough to drown the vicar in the hymns.' 'And your organist and the choirmaster won't be here?' I queried. Alfie shrugged. 'Mr Grinder's a nervous wreck today,' he explained in a matter-of-fact voice. 'He gets to be a nervous wreck sometimes when the vicar gets too enthusiastic about singing at the services – and last night he actually came to choir practice as well – so Mr Grinder's a nervous wreck today, and you can't do weddings when you're a nervous wreck, can you?' A loud, cheerful voice sounded and a young man in a tracksuit trotted into the

6

vestry beaming smiles in all directions. 'That's the vicar,' Alfie informed me *sotto voce*. 'He's always like that when he comes in, ever so jovial.' The vicar hastily buttoned his shirt collar and slipped into it a strip of white plastic, presumably representing a clerical collar. Bundling himself into his cassock and surplice he strode among us, reminding us what a joy it was for us all to join in the happiness of a wedding. It was a pity that there had been a little mix-up over the date of the wedding but, after all, it was the ladies' special day and they all had so much to do.

The young vicar's attitude to hopeless muck-ups was so infectious that the choirmen who'd had to forgo their presence at the day's vital local football match and the ladies who had to delay their time with their horses all forgot to grumble, and the choir gave a rumbustious account of themselves at the service. The vicar, generous and helpful to a fault, sang 'Praise my soul' more heartily than ever before. Sir John Goss would not have recognized his tune, of course, but Goss the Boxer became fascinated to the extent that he never took his eyes off the vicar during the entire singing of the hymn.

Certainly the whole jolly wedding service went off without a hitch from the bride's entrance, with Archie raging away with 'Colonel Bogey' with all the stops out, to the final procession down the main aisle with heroic deafening excerpts from 'The Twilight of the Gods'. Somewhere up in the tower the bell-ringers were adding riotously to the general excitement as the wedding party were marshalled all over the place by the photographers until the 'happy couple' eventually escaped, borne away in a gleaming carriage drawn by two of the local brewery's champion Shire horses.

Back in the vestry where the choir were disrobing, the vicar bounced among us full of the joys of the wedding. 'He's a genuine jolly person,' Archie enthused. 'He's just as jolly after funerals as well, and when he's been able to slip one of his latest pop praise songs into choral Matins at the last minute.'

The vicar barged into us. 'Such a pity Mr Grinder missed the service. He would have *revelled* in our singing. I certainly found myself singing *exuberantly*! But he won't miss out altogether. I've taped the whole service and I'll take it round to him this evening. He's especially fond of "Praise, my soul, the King of heaven". Isn't he? That'll cheer him up!'

My train acquaintance, one of the last of the Mohicans, was hovering nearby. The wonderful comical smile was still there. 'That definitely means no choir practice this week,' he piped. 'Old Grinder won't be recovered by Friday!'

2

The Big Clean-up

It is always a joy to escape for a few days into the cosily detached world of my friend George's Berkshire village. Miraculously it remains a perfect example of the storybook village. It houses no city commuters, the powers-that-be have no plans for carving a six-lane motorway through its centre, no one has thought of modernizing by closing the local infants' school and the sub-post office, and the single-line railway station is still fully operational with a real live porter. Furthermore, the church and the pub still splendidly fulfil their ancient functions, thus making the notion of a modern purpose-built community centre quite unthinkable.

In company with other timeless traditions, the church choir practice is on Fridays. During early evening, members start drifting towards the church vestry and when enough have arrived to raise a reasonable racket, the organist, an always immaculately, sportingly attired local Don Juan with a roguish grin, accompanies them through the bawling of some familiar hymns and psalms, and pays his usual extravagant compliments on the singing of the choir's bunch of remarkably attractive choirgirls. Then they all retire next door to the pub for the rest of the evening.

One Friday evening recently I arrived in the village for a few days' stay with George. As usual I had intended to drop in on choir practice in preparation for my customary 'guest appearance' in the choir on the Sunday. However, owing to certain insurmountable difficulties being experienced by the railway people in London, I arrived late to find that choir practice had finished and everybody was in the Barley Mow. At this stage of the evening only the vicar, a huge man with a fog-horn voice, could actually make himself clearly heard above the roar of everyone arguing with everyone else at once, and as I entered the snug he was leaning back over the counter in the well-known manner in which he leaned back over the pulpit Sunday by Sunday, as he prepared to thunder forth his sermon before the congregation had a chance to settle down and close their eyes. 'Friends,' he roared, 'mates – don't forget it's cleaning-up day in the church and churchyard tomorrow. See you all in the morning at half-past seven onwards.'

'He'll be there half-past eleven onwards,' remarked George to me. 'But he's *good*! He can get everyone slogging away for *hours* before he even gets out of bed. It's the way he says things. He really is good.'

I hadn't been present at a cleaning-up day before. 'Do the choir take part in all this?' I asked. 'Take part? Yes! Good heavens, yes,' George assured me. 'We're all there the whole time – most important.'

I must admit I was a little surprised at this enthusiasm as many of the choirs I knew never did anything the vicar wanted them to do, mainly because they backed the organist who was always crossing swords with the vicar about hymn tunes and about choir members reading

Sunday papers and making noises during the sermon. However, there was obviously no dissension here, and when I arrived at the church early on Saturday morning I had no difficulty in spotting the members of the choir among the dozens of parishioners who were trampling all over the churchyard with lawn mowers and rakes and pots of flowers, and planting ladders and buckets of water in each other's way in the church. The choir were keeping well out of the way, sitting quietly in corners and doing absolutely nothing – except for the Don Juan organist, who was sitting at the organ reading the paper and consuming a cheese roll that looked like half a loaf.

'What do I do?' I asked George, who was lounging contemplatively in a choir stall as the ladders and buckets surged by and a suffocating smell of sprayed furniture polish and disinfectant assailed us from all sides. 'Ah! You can be very helpful,' he said. 'The choir are spread a little thin on the ground at the moment. Could you go and sit over there?' and he indicated the opposite choir stall.

'Right,' I said briskly, 'and what do I do?'

'Do?' he echoed. 'What *all* the choir are doing. It's most important.'

I looked around. 'But they're not *doing* anything,' I said.

'Not *doing* anything?' He looked aggrieved. 'We're *watching*. We're keeping our eyes on our things. I can tell you, if we don't keep our eyes like hawks on this lot they'll throw out everything in the choir vestry and the stalls – even in the organ loft, so that on Sunday morning and for weeks afterwards we won't be able to find a thing. At last year's cleaning I was just in time to stop some busybody parcelling up a whole batch of anthems for waste-paper collection, and I caught a woman actually trying to stuff my cassock into a rag bag.' George looked indignant. 'I've had that cassock for years and years – only fit for the rag bag indeed!'

I felt rather self-conscious sitting in the stall in the midst of all the frantic hubbub of work so I started looking through a battered hymn book with its cover barely clinging to the spine. Suddenly a large lady with a businesslike expression and a broom appeared at one end of the stall and started sweeping me towards the other end, where a similar large lady started spraying me with polish. 'I'll take that,' she announced as she pushed me out of the way and grabbed the hymn book. 'The choir always leave these all over the place and this one needs repairing anyway. We really can't go on like this.'

'Are you good at cleaning brass? – of course you are!' The vicar's wife abruptly appeared at my elbow. She thrust some rubber gloves and a tin of brass-cleaner and a duster at me. 'The memorial plaques are on the wall over there.' She pointed, beamed at me and bustled off.

I felt the eyes of the entire choir on me as I donned the rubber gloves and went to inspect the plaques. They were mostly late-Victorian with gothic lettering and gave glowing accounts of the lives of various local worthies whose lavish, angel-laden tombs littered the churchyard and made the new curate quite depressed. George had told me that the young man was intensely artistic in a sort of outlandish, medieval way and it upset him no end to see the line of graceless stone 'packing cases' marching right up to the beautiful fifteenth-century church doorway, every time he came to conduct Evensong. George said the tombs put the curate in quite the wrong frame of mind for worship and spoilt his dinner into the bargain. He reckoned the sight of them was even more shattering to his nerves than when the choir so obviously revelled in singing some awful sentimental Victorian hymn just before the blessing.

By mid-morning I had polished a row of half-a-dozen brass plaques and was rather proud of the way they reflected what the young medievally inclined curate apparently called the 'frightful, garish' blues and reds of the Victorian windows, which glowed in the summer sun with a blatant disregard for his tender sensibilities.

The curate had dutifully arrived by this time and now moved bravely between the frightful stained-glass windows and – to use his oft repeated words – the elephantine Victorian pews that *utterly* obliterated the lovely proportions of the medieval nave. He hovered and smiled bravely at the workers, even when they were not looking at him and hadn't noticed him. Back in the church porch he paused momentarily to regard a large, round child who was totally immersed in the task of chalking funny faces on a displayed Tudor tombstone. Then he wandered out sadly into the sunlight and was gone.

The vicar was of course quite different. Everybody saw and heard him as he tramped into the church sharp at 11.30 shouting 'Good', 'Splendid', 'Great', and 'Terrific mates!' Some grime-covered, dishevelled workers started to show him what they had done, and the lady who had swept me out of the choir stall thrust a broom into his hand with an irresistible smile. The vicar said 'Great', and started with flamboyant vigour to scatter a pile of swept-up dust and choir debris all over the chancel floor, which had already been swept and polished. He then waved the broom in a jolly gesture at the dangerously swaying figure of the vicar's warden, who was attending to a light-fitting at the top of a particularly rickety ladder, and announced that he had to tear himself away to interview a couple who wanted to get married.

Having completed my allotted task, I made my way to the choir vestry. It was quiet and still in there. No worker greeted me – just our bass soloist who raised his eyes to heaven from the sporting pages of his tabloid, boomed, 'What a morning,' and returned to his tabloid. Two other choir 'guards', playing chess on a miniature board in a dark corner, were too engrossed to notice. Tottering piles of yellowing anthem copies and settings cascaded around them on every available surface, battered hymn books and coverless psalters bulged from dusty crevices and corners. The veteran vestry piano was loaded down with a tangle of cassocks and surplices, flung there after the latest Evensong, where the wearers would know precisely where to find them when they blundered into the vestry two minutes before the next Sunday's Matins. A touch of romance had been introduced, doubtless by one of Don Juan's attractive choirgirls, in the shape of a heart and arrow motif lip-sticked onto the spotty vestry mirror.

Don Juan himself now appeared from the organ, brushing crumbs from his sporty attire. 'They'll be swarming in here upsetting everything soon,' he warned, gazing through the doorway at the toiling workers in the nave and chancel. He took a few stealthy steps towards a nearby pew and retrieved a broom abandoned there, perhaps, by some backsliding worker who, like the vicar, had suddenly realized that he or she was urgently needed somewhere else. He swept some churchyard grit, a few sweet-papers and two bent drawing-pins under a chair that was leaning against the wall on its last legs, and righted a sepia picture of a particularly sinister-looking Victorian vicar that was hanging at a drunken angle over the piano. 'There,' he said confidently, 'they'll go away now that things are already tidied up here.'

A small, perspiring man wearing wide red braces and shoes with dusters tied round them peeped in at the door, clinging to a bedraggled mop. The organist greeted him cheerfully. 'All done in here,' he said, beaming at the unbelievable chaos behind him. 'All nice and tidy. You go and have a nice cup of tea.' The little man gaped, looked puzzled, then bewildered. Then he grinned and, to my surprise, winked. 'Yes, I see,' he said. 'I'll tell the others.'

The broom-wielding, polish-spraying ladies, whom I had earlier encountered – 'the leaders of the wrecking crew' as the organist called them – proved rather more difficult to repel than he of the red braces, but repel them we did, the bass soloist, the organist, the miniature-chess players and I, and at last, late in the afternoon, all was peace and quiet and bright and gleaming in the church (just peace and quiet in the choir vestry).

The next morning at choral Matins the vicar said he felt that they could *all* congratulate themselves on a good job well done – he had certainly enjoyed the experience. He was sorry that most of the congregation had got no hymn books this morning but he felt sure the sidesmen would soon lay their hands on them – the hymn books, of course, not the congregation. It was just that in the reorganization they had been tidied away to a more con-venient place – and did anyone happen to know where the collection bags were?

In the choir vestry we'd collected our hymn books and psalters as usual from secluded crevices and corners, and we'd known exactly where to locate our cassocks and surplices in the tangle atop the vestry piano. Here, at least, life continued on its serene way. Even the sinister Victorian vicar had slipped back to his accustomed drunken angle.

3

Disgusting

It was a hot Sunday morning, in August, in the choir vestry of the village church where my friend Felix runs the choir and coaxes the most alarming sounds out of the brutish organ. The vestry door was open wide, offering a close-up view of the churchyard rubbish-dump and a line of rusting dustbins bursting with dead flowers and empty wine bottles. Felix's disgraceful wreck of a bike leaned among it all, and a gentle simmering breeze occasionally puffed a unique rural odour into the vestry.

Felix sat at the piano sorting copies of the morning's anthem that were beyond repair, from those that could still be held without actually disintegrating in the hand, and the only other occupant of the vestry, apart from me, was a small, agitated, indescribably untidy-looking choir-boy enveloped in a cassock several sizes too large for him, with half the buttons missing. 'I can't find my surplice,' he complained to Felix. 'Someone's always pinching it.'

'You ought to be pleased,' said Felix. 'I wouldn't like to be seen wearing a thing like your surplice. It's always filthy and all screwed up – doesn't your mother wash and iron?'

'She says it's no good washing it,' explained the choir-boy. 'She says nothing keeps clean here because the vestry's never cleaned.'

'Rubbish,' said Felix dismissively, rising and upsetting an overflowing ashtray all over the piano. 'Here, take these anthems and put them out in the choir stalls.' The boy took up the limp music copies. 'These look a hundred years old,' he said – 'like my surplice.' 'They *are* a hundred years old,' confirmed Felix. 'Your surplice is not a hundred years old, Ernie, it's just filthy.'

By contrast with the majority of Felix's choirboys, his teenaged choirgirls always looked most attractive. Two of them now entered the vestry – an immaculate blonde and a striking redhead.

'You look disgusting,' said the blonde to the choirboy. 'You always are disgusting.'

'I've lost my surplice,' said Ernie.

'It's just where you left it after Evensong last Sunday,' supplied the redhead. 'I can see it sticking out from under the piano. Felix has got his heel on it.'

Three more choirboys erupted into the vestry now. They were just as awful-looking as Ernie and, from what I remembered, were wont to wear surplices in very much the same outrageous condition as his. By common consent they all joined in a sort of violent wrestling match in the cassock cupboard. The blonde turned to me in icy disgust. 'I don't know why we have them in the choir,' she said. 'No wonder we always come bottom in the music festival. What do they expect with that lot?'

'It's because of our Christmas outing,' explained the redhead in rather warmer tones. She smiled at me beguilingly. 'We have quite a do for the choir every Christmas, you know. We go to London for dinner and a show – no expense spared. We get the money from three or four of those old ladies who sit in the front pews – they're the ones who keep on complaining that the choirgirls wear too much jewellery in church.' 'Cheap jewellery,' corrected the icy blonde. 'They are on about too much *cheap* jewellery.'

'The earrings I wore last Sunday weren't cheap,' returned the redhead spiritedly – 'not even in the sale.'

'No, but they were rather big,' observed the blonde, 'and they sparkled, and the ladies said they distracted the vicar when he was singing the versicles.'

'Anyway,' resumed the redhead, deftly straightening my surplice and enveloping me in a drift of exotic perfume, 'these women who give the money simply dote on the choirboys. They think they're sweet and that you can't have a real church choir without them. If the lot of them got thrown out that would be the end of our Christmas outings – definitely. And nobody would want that.'

'Our new vicar would,' retorted the icy blonde firmly. 'My father says the vicar doesn't like anything that was organized before he came here, especially if it's working well. He says he's even trying to change the rules of the parish men's club so that women can join. He says a men's club is sexist and doesn't fit in with the idea of the Church being one united family.'

'My mum likes to get my dad out from under her feet at the men's club,' said the redhead. 'She likes the men's club.'

'My father says it's because the vicar's new and you always have trouble with new vicars,' explained the blonde. 'He says they all have a sort of grand design with our choir.'

'Or the Christmas outing,' said the redhead hopefully.

'Or the Christmas outing,' assured the blonde.

This new vicar at Felix's church is *very* new. He still likes to feel he is the supremo. Not for him endless parish discussions and consultative committees and suggestion boxes. He is sublimely sure that the parish needs, and indeed fully appreciates, a strong decisive leader, an unfettered director. He likes to feel that, as vicar, he is fully in charge of everything. He particularly likes to feel he is fully in charge of the choir. The choir, too, like him to feel that he is fully in charge of them. That way he is much less trouble – much less likely to get upset over their singing and to request them to stay for 'some words of guidance and warning' on hot Sunday evenings after Evensong, when they are all anxious to get away to do whatever choirs do on hot summer evenings after Evensong.

The vicar regards his relationship with the choir as very satisfactory. Each Friday evening he turns up at choir practice and takes over from Felix every few minutes with instructions of how best to sing the hymns and psalms and, indeed, what hymns and psalms to sing and what verses he doesn't approve of and that therefore must be left out. Felix is very attentive and follows the vicar's interruptions with serious-voiced remarks like 'Now have you got that, ladies and gentlemen?' and 'Now the vicar has made that very clear, let us make sure we remember.' Sometimes he will ask the vicar 'Could you just repeat that? It is so important that we get it exactly right.' Then, with an expression of gratitude on his face approaching the idiotic, he thanks the vicar for again giving up so much of his precious time for the benefit of the choir, and the vicar says something about the pursuit of perfection always being worth unstinted effort and the selfless sacrifice of any amount of one's precious time, and strides home with a joyful heart.

The choir then settle down to practise the music precisely as they've done for years and years. And the vicar, being completely unmusical, is comfortably certain that they are singing precisely as he had instructed, so everyone is satisfied and happy with what is going on and, in the words of Felix, they rip through the service like a house on fire.

On that hot Sunday morning I was a guest of Felix's artful choir on the occasion of a special celebratory choral Matins in honour of the 50 unbroken years' service of one of the choirmen. He was very small and wiry and always sat at the extreme end of a choir stall, half hidden behind a pillar that supported a strikingly ornate brass lamp that hadn't worked since they'd converted it from gas to electricity 50 years ago. It was said that he'd never missed a service, and he was considered the backbone of the choir although no one was quite certain what kind of voice he had because, during the course of any singing, he appeared to be totally involved in shuffling his music and finding the wrong hymn in the wrong hymn book. He was called Ed by everyone in the choir, although the new vicar, who had not yet learned his name, called him 'old chap', and Ed called *him* the worst vicar they'd ever had – a description he'd applied to the last six vicars. He also averred that Felix was the worst organist they'd ever had, having been part of the package when the church had salvaged the organ from the derelict 'silent' cinema before the Second World War.

The vicar was continually occupied with the mechanics of vital leadership, which included churning out on his home printer an endless stream of new 'praise songs' (so much more relevant to today's yearnings and needs than the 'pie-in-the-sky' Victorian hymns in the official hymn books) and plans for ripping out the church's oak pews and replacing them with nice, bright, orange plastic chairs. He looked urgently, enthusiastically to the future. He really had no time at all for remembering the past. But the choirman's achievement of 'sticking' it in the choir for 50 years had needed a bit of doing, he supposed, although he could not help noticing that the choir people tended to do that kind of thing quite a lot. They appeared to have no spirit of adventure, no call to travel onwards and develop the vital Christian life. In fact they didn't seem to be vital at all. They just joined the choir at an early age and stayed there for the rest of their lives, demanding everything to remain the same and bawling the same hymns and refusing to 'see the light' from the kindly leadership of new vicar after new vicar who burst upon the parish, each full of jolly back-slapping companionship and plans to alter everything the previous jolly back-slapping vicar had imposed.

So, much out of character, feeling almost a guilty turncoat, the present vicar had brought himself to join the choir and congregation in the church hall after the service and to do what was expected of him in presenting the choir's longest-serving member with a gold wristwatch and a large framed photograph of the whole choir taken outside a villainous-looking Victorian pub on the occasion of their latest summer outing to the south coast.

At a presentation such as this, people always talked about the past and kept on bringing in references to 'the good old days' and those happy times – which depressed

22

the vicar mightily; so much so that, having handed over the gifts and got the recipient's name wrong twice in his few words about dedication and achievement, he stopped abruptly, slapped a few bystanders on the back, said, 'Good! Marvellous! Great!' to no one in particular, and disappeared.

The immaculate blonde and the redhead were suddenly pushed against me in the ensuing rush for the free drinks. The blonde stood facing me and to my consternation her voice was even more icy than it had been in the vestry. The blue eyes flashed. 'You are disgusting,' she said. I looked down puzzled, abashed, and then saw where her eyes were really focused. Ernie, the choirboy with the ill-fitting garments, had crept from under a table and was expertly tying one of my ankles to a chair. Felix arrived clutching a foaming tankard and grinning. 'The vicar's just had a word with me. He says he's had some serious complaints about the boys' behaviour – says that if they don't improve he'll have to suspend the lot of them.'

'What! Our boys suspended?' gasped the redhead. 'Not likely! He can't interfere with the choir like that. Cheek!'

The blonde dragged Ernie squirming from under the table and cuffed him expertly. 'Threatening our boys, is he!' she trilled. 'Who does he think he is? Disgusting!'

4

The One-off Church

This is a story of tradition – ancient and curious, odd and untimely – that still holds together some valiant village church choirs of the old school.

The cosy English village where my friend Charlie has the good fortune to live, and growl deepest bass in the church choir, is very much in the style of those make-believe rural neighbourhoods beloved of writers of crime fiction – smiling, rustic havens of peace and tranquillity that are secretly seething cauldrons of every kind of crime imaginable, requiring the permanent presence of a peerless private eye who regularly, and hugely successfully, sorts out the endless stream of villains.

But in one respect Charlie's village is unique. It lacks the usual picture-postcard village church that, with the village pub, is generally the centre of attention for visitors. Fear not, however, there *is* a village church. It's a converted eighteenth-century barn which was architecturally most unsuitable for conversion. Nevertheless, the mid-Victorian local builder had made a good job of it in the circumstances, and all had gone well at the new church's opening, with a full, very 'proper' congregation on the ground floor and a specially press-ganged choir from the usual Saturday-night riotous songsters of the

Fox and Ferret (regarded by members of the 'proper' congregation who *never* sang, even in church, as disgusting) crammed onto a platform that stuck out like a large, open drawer halfway up an inside back wall of the barn. This platform was, of course, called the gallery, and it supported a hefty oak choir stall adorned with a threatening-looking carved wood head, said to represent that of the vicar. Charlie, however, is adamant that such a villainous visage could surely have had nothing to do with the vicar of that time and is almost certainly that of the then choirmaster – some choirmasters, Charlie explains, have artistic temperaments that are liable to become very dominant and affect their facial expressions, which can be very awkward for choirs, particularly those who can't read music and bawl everything at full blast in the Saturday-night bar manner, with no respect for what the composer or choirmaster had in mind.

This choir stall is a special one, donated to the barn church in memory of a former village inn-keeper who had, for many years before the advent of the church, let the villagers use the back room of the Fox and Ferret for Sunday morning services, hopefully to be followed by prolonged congregational get-togethers in the front bar. Needless to say, this second part of the Sunday morning arrangement had never met with any degree of success owing to the fact that the men of the congregation were normally accompanied by their wives and children and had to ignore the delights of the front bar.

And, still with the choir stall – for reasons lost in the mists of time – no provision was made for the choir to reach the gallery from the interior of the church and members had to clamber up a perilous flight of wooden steps halfway up an outer wall of the barn. Popular rumour had it that the very 'proper' congregation were most appreciative of this circumstance because the Saturday-night revellers' choir from the Fox and Ferret, although unfortunately necessary, were hardly the kind of individuals to come into too close contact with the genteel members of the congregation. You had to draw the line somewhere and, as Charlie says, segregated singers was the answer.

For the rest of the nineteenth century the situation concerning the choir's external entry into the church continued happily as a tradition. Then, to celebrate the opening of the twentieth century, a well-respected member of the congregation, who'd made a fortune in earlier years selling obscenely overpriced rails to the new railway companies, decided that he could no longer put up with the weekly nerve-grinding cacophony from the choir and presented the church with an organ large and powerful enough for a cathedral, capable of drowning the choir and uplifting his tender spirit. Needless to say, however, this expensive plan to diminish the choir sound was an utter failure because the organist jubilantly joined forces with the choir and, as Charlie put it, unmusically, highlighted the raucous bawling and regularly raised the roof.

And today the age-old, loyally upholding, traditionally English division between congregation and choir still quietly exists, although during the past few years somewhat modified by the appearance in the gallery of choir ladies, particularly young ones who sport jeans and large off-white trainers and T-shirts lauding football teams or advertising someone's Old Time cider. Everyone is an enthusiastic member of the choir and supporter of the organist even if, like the rest of the choir, they cheerfully ignore his words of wisdom every choir-practice night.

The present organist and choirmaster is not one of those with an agonizing artistic temperament, so he doesn't suffer at all from the circumstance that he has to clamber up the outside wall with the choir to get to the organ loft in the gallery. A cheerful, easygoing bachelor who is quite content to put up with the young vicar's constant pop 'praise songs' suggestions in place of traditional hymns and the 'confounded noisy organ and choir hooligans' complaints of the retired major who reads the first lesson at Matins and whose lavish generosity keeps the village church going comfortably his way. This organist is even happy to endure the burden of conducting choir practice every Friday night for the huge privilege of having control of one of the only church organs for miles that is not falling to bits for lack of funds and organists.

Very recently I spent a most enjoyable weekend with Charlie and his wife, who treated me to a conducted tour of their unique village church. As we turned a corner from behind the huge listed building which is the vicarage, there suddenly, startlingly, was the barn church with sight of a spidery figure hurrying jerkily halfway up a blank wall to a single narrow door. The wooden steps were hardly noticeable. 'That's our organist,' Charlie told me, rather proudly I thought. 'He looks like a spider up there,' I said. Charlie agreed. 'But he's an ideal spider for us, he sort of *unites* us in the gallery – and he conducts our singing at football matches. One or two of us can read music now, too.'

By the time we'd entered the church through the main (congregational) entrance, taking note of instructions chalked on a school blackboard in the porch (Please wipe your boots. Keep dogs on leads. Don't take away the pew cushions), the organist had climbed into the organ loft in the gallery and was shouting down to a party of men surrounding what appeared to be a box-like wooden structure on stilts in the gangway between the pews. Charlie explained what was going on. 'They're doing a vital job here. Y'see, we've never had a pulpit in the church. The vicar just plods about on a spare piece of floor in front of the congregation and does the preaching bit, but now there's one or two fussy people who feel he should have a pulpit so that he can be seen by everybody and make more use of his gestures and general acting ability. He's a very gifted vicar, y'see – runs the local drama club as well as the church and the horse–boat cruises on the canal.'

One of the men in the church wedged a long ladder against a fat wooden pillar next to the pulpit. From the gallery the organist instructed, 'Now go up as far as you can and tell me when you can see me up here reading a paper.' The man climbed halfway up the ladder and stopped abruptly. 'This is it,' he shouted excitedly. 'I can see you sittin' there reading a paper.' The organist shouted down again, 'Right! Good! Now go down again till you can't see me at all, or my paper.' The man followed his instructions from on high and suddenly halted again, confirming, 'OK, you've gone!'

Charlie explained the puzzling procedure to me. 'Y'see, the vicar preaches the same sermon at both the morning and evening services, which means the choir are exposed to all this *repetition* – well, we can put up with a one-off sermon but if we've got to sit through the same one again in the evening – well. I meantersay!' Charlie paused to let the awful fact sink in. 'Well, of course we've never put up with that, so during the Sunday morning service we peruse our Sunday papers while the vicar's having his say because we know we'll be able to hear it all at Evensong. We've gone on like this for years – never falling asleep behind a pillar like some of the congregation.' Charlie sighed. 'Now the whole tradition is threatened because of this pulpit business. Standing on the floor down there the vicar can't see into the gallery, but a pulpit might bring him nearly level with us. The whole idea is unthinkable!' I made suitable indignant noises and he went on in happier tones. 'We think we'll be all right though. We're making sure the new pulpit – well, that box on legs – will not be *too* tall. The carpenter who's got the job is one of our choirmen y'see – a very unsettling, piercing male alto he is, keeps the choir careering along at a cracking pace right through the service – he'll see the pulpit is just high enough to let the vicar pinpoint any sleeping malingerers in the congregation – a disrespectful, disgusting practice.'

'Whereas,' I said, 'the choir reading papers during the morning service is OK?'

Charlie spoke warmly. 'A respected quaint old tradition. The choir never misses the sermon. It ensures that we all turn up for Evensong. United we stand! It's our tradition!'

5

A Glorious Opportunity

When an experienced vicar advertises for a colleague, he or she always mentions the unique and glorious opportunities that the parish offers to the right person for converting the hordes of local heathen. Also described glowingly are the homely comforts of the worm-eaten Victorian barn ('now ready and waiting') to which the colleague can repair when not doing the converting.

If the vicar is particularly worldly and doesn't mind stretching a point, a line is sometimes added hinting at generous Easter Offerings.

But the advertiser never mentions the choir. This is because choirs really upset vicars. There is always some sort of trouble connected with choirs. Either they are so powerful – in voice and influence – that the priest can't be heard, or else there isn't one at all, and the priest has an awful job droning through Merbecke with two or three servers.

At the village church where I recently sang, they had just passed from the latter to the former state. A new vicar, who was so young that he still believed that all church councillors and choristers were Christian ladies and gentlemen, had made strenuous efforts to form a choir, and these now seemed to be bearing some kind of fruit.

The newly recruited singers, two dozen strong, were all people who had had church-choir experience and had left their previous posts for the usual reasons – the advent of a new spouse, vicar, organist, or hymn book. And each had his or her own firmly entrenched idea of how the choir should be run. The organist, on the other hand, had no idea whatsoever, but as he didn't want to upset anyone at this vital stage, he wasn't unduly worried.

In the choir vestry, before Matins, the choir members were standing around in a number of clearly defined groups, regarding each other suspiciously, and speaking in low, tense tones. In the first few weeks of their corporate existence much of the vicar's enthusiasm had affected the members and they had really worked hard at creating a friendly atmosphere and getting to know each other's views on the type of music that should be sung. This, of course, had been most helpful, and in no time at all had enabled them to split into their opinion groups and oppose each other very effectively.

The vicar introduced me to the nearest group and then blundered on, heartily butting into the other groups and saying how pleased he was to see such a splendid attendance – such unity of purpose, he called it. My group's main support, I soon learned, was for *Hymns A & M* and 'Amens' at the end of every hymn, so I felt quite at home. Of course, I was lucky. I might just as easily have been delivered to the next lot, who stood for the *English Hymnal* and no 'Amens' at all. Then there were the small group who were horrified at the thought of anything but plainsong, and the much larger group who were horrified at the thought of plainsong and supported *Moody & Sankey*. There were also a group who wanted a brass band instead of the organ, but no one took them very seriously.

When we took up our positions in the chancel, I was placed at the top of a choir stall next to our group leader, but I couldn't at first identify my neighbour below me, or indeed anyone else in the stall, owing to the presence of an outsized Saxon pillar which stood fatly by my side and appeared to support nothing but a hymn board. At the commencement of the first hymn, however, my neighbour revealed himself. He was obviously one of an opposition group, for he held an *English Hymnal* proudly at arm's length, and kept on peeping round the pillar and glaring at my *Ancient & Modern* as he bellowed what he clearly regarded as the correct version of 'Captains of the saintly band'.

A sudden thought struck me and I looked across at the vicar. With head lifted high, he was singing the famous hymn with all the uninhibited enthusiasm of the very young and untrained. And he held no book at all.

My eye next wandered to the organist. Had he declared himself? But he was smart also. The venerable green curtain, which had obviously hung there before anyone had even thought of *A & M* or *English Hymnal*, was drawn tightly behind the console, and hid everything except a flypaper, which dangled delicately from above. And judging by what he was playing, it seemed improbable that the maestro was using either of the accepted hymn books. From his magnificently devil-may-care rendering, I imagined he was using one of those music rolls that operate roundabout organs.

Anyway, the service rolled along quite well. Naturally, the congregation looked a little puzzled. After all, they had not been used to a choir for many years, and didn't immediately appreciate such a nerve-shattering sound every time the vicar announced a hymn. But they came into their own when we reached the psalms. Even the vicar had not yet fooled himself into risking half-a-dozen different pointings of the psalms all sung at once, so they were still said. He led the way, and the congregation followed obediently with all the mumbled incoherence which distinguishes the Church of England.

The choir didn't follow at all. In the revered tradition of church choirs they obviously considered that spoken parts of the service had nothing to do with them. Some started to find the next hymn; others studied intently the damp patches on the chancel ceiling; and one man leaned over to the boys' stall and confiscated a half-eaten sausage roll and a noisy bag of crisps.

In conversation after the service the vicar told me that the activities in the parish were expanding so happily that he would soon be needing a colleague. I saw his advertisement a few weeks later. He mentioned the usual heathen and home comforts, but then his inexperience showed itself. 'Large and enthusiastic choir,' he had written.

6

Matins Like a Football Final

I was in the process of planning a magazine article on the present-day state of small-town and village church choirs. A depressing account in a church newspaper, in which the writer had claimed that it was near impossible these days to recruit singers for such choirs, had provoked me into, hopefully, redressing the balance of the situation. I decided to seek out one of the choirs mentioned in the article and discover a few points for myself. Since, however, I was quite unacquainted with the West Country area of my chosen church, I got in touch with a one time business acquaintance who, I realized, lived in the vicinity and was, I believed, a local church chorister.

Arthur was most enthusiastic about 'filling me in' on his small, very attractive country town – 'Well, hardly a town at all – rather, a big lively village – a big *lively* musical village.' His obvious overriding interest in the musical aspect was immediate as he quickly dismissed other features of the area as 'the best patch around for miles' and 'just the job'.

We'd met after work in a coffee bar near St Paul's Cathedral and Arthur, without consulting me, plonked down on our table two huge mugs of hot, almost black liquid topped with melting puffy white foam, and continued talking vigorously. 'It's a fact, y'see, almost *every* family in the place has a musical tradition going back for generations. Nearly everyone plays an instrument or sings or composes, and we've got enough talent to support a junior orchestra and a champion brass band *and* the "top drawer" choir of Holy Trinity church.' Arthur whisked the white puffy stuff into the black substance in his mug. 'I'm in Holy Trinity choir. It's a great honour for me, because I think my voice is nothing special so I don't sing solos. We regularly sweep the board at the county music festival and we've put out some first-rate CDs. We've also got an unwritten understanding with our vicar that he doesn't sing with us during the services.' Apparently the vicar fully understood that the beauty and balance of the superb choir's performance would be utterly lost beneath his hoarse, football hooligan bellow. And as for the congregation, Holy Trinity is one of those churches where, if an unsuspecting stranger, thrilled by its gothic splendour, decided to stay for church evensong and starts joining in the singing of 'Glorious things of Thee are spoken' in a hearty have-a-go voice, he or she is immediately menaced with startled, outraged glares, causing the insensitive intruder to immediately lose voice and sidle along the pew to the shelter of a convenient pillar.

Arthur paused for a moment to finish what still lurked of the murky mixture that remained in his coffee mug, and I indicated how impressed I was with the loyally nurtured perfection of his choir. 'But yours is not the choir I read about in the newspaper article,' I said. 'There must be another one in this district.'

Arthur smiled broadly and spoke affectionately. 'Oh, yes, there certainly is. That's the parish church choir – the Dust Bin.'

'The Dust Bin!' After so many years' experience, I'm not exactly shocked at what some choirs good-humouredly call other choirs, but the Dust Bin ...

Arthur clarified. 'Yes, that's what we at Holy Trinity call them. Y'see, with all these musical families around here, there are always a few members whose voices don't quite measure up and they get left behind, but the tradition must be maintained so these types don't get ignored – they get shunted down to the parish church choir. There's our choirmaster's daughter, for instance – a charming girl who looks good in the choir – she's been banished to the parish church choir and she loves it. They've got the biggest choir for miles down at the parish church. Anybody can join, there's never any auditions and they have Friday-night choir practice in the back room of the Red Lion because their organist reckons the choir vestry is too small for so many singers and the thunderous blunders they make at full blast. They're a very enthusiastic choir, y'see. Well they have to be really – the bell-ringers are the trouble. They're always forgetting to hold up when the service begins and are often clanging away right through the first hymn. The choir have to be loud to drown out that lot, I can tell you!'

I was intrigued. 'And what about their organist?' I asked. 'How does he cope?'

'Now, there's a happy man,' Arthur assured me. 'In his young days he was a super-cinema organist and used to get hundreds of audience bawling "Land of hope and glory" and "Roll out the barrel" when the usherettes were selling chocolates and cigarettes in the programme interval between the big picture and the supporting picture.'

'He must miss those days,' I said. Arthur beamed. 'Oh no, not really. With him on the organ bolstering up the parish church choir, he gets the congregation raising the roof. It sounds like a football final at choral Matins!'

I appreciated Arthur's generous efforts at enthusiasm and delight for the parish church choir, coming from a member of the elite Holy Trinity choir who were obviously untouched by the parish church choir's vandalism of sacred music. 'They certainly seem to be a marvellous lot, the parish church choir,' I said, 'but again, they can't be the choir who were in my newspaper article about choirs who can't find singers.' Arthur grinned. 'Ah, I think I have the answer to that one. The parish church choir contains all the members of the Red Lion district darts club. The Sunday on which the man from the newspaper came there was a date muddle. Nearly all the choir were at the final of the district championship, which they always win, and the only people in the choir stalls were two veteran contraltos who declined to chat with a nosy reporter who nevertheless said how much he admired this tiny choir of two in these hard times and gave them a special mention in his article.'

Arthur said it's funny how things turn out. A third church became involved in the local choir situation. After a very long wait an historical church just outside the bounds of Arthur's village was about to have a resident choirmaster. A young music teacher who had recently joined the local church school moved in next door to the vestry. The young man was a shining enthusiast for choral singing and immediately after his first visit to choral Matins in the church, where the choir stalls were entirely empty and the sound of singing from the congregation was slightly below the hum of a couple of lazy bumble bees, he immediately volunteered to raise a choir worthy of this gem of a perfect Norman church. With the backing of the priest-in-charge, also a young musical man, who played the flute, the new choirmaster gathered a surprisingly large number of would-be choristers for a first rehearsal. He didn't introduce much actual music but talked interestedly of wonderful possibilities for a choir going on to concerts or choral festivals.

He wore throughout an eager sparkling grin, which drew in volunteers for the next few weeks. Then came talk of auditions and wonderful medieval music, nothing like the – well, friends, rather awful Victorian hymns in your hymn books which we must certainly change as soon as possible.

Some of the choir volunteers began to waver. They hadn't been singing much over the year but they did like many of the old favourites in their hymn books – and what was all this about medieval music and *new* hymn books?

Nevertheless, a goodly number of volunteers presented themselves for the auditions and at the end of the session the new choirmaster was delighted with the outcome. 'Eight singers!' he enthused. 'Eight singers who will put our church on the music map!' But the new choirmaster didn't forsake the unsuccessful volunteers. 'Every one of you has the potential to – er – let your voice be heard – and I'll tell you just how to do it. There's a sure way for singers like you.'

Recently, down at the parish church, the choir has swelled so much that they've crammed in another choir stall and ordered more cassocks and surplices and the jubilant organist has arranged for a much larger room for rehearsals at the Red Lion.

In ever increasing numbers, people planning for excessively enthusiastic, very loud and colourful wedding ceremonies have been choosing the parish church, and the parish church choir sings whatever they want and raises the roof on the big day. As their jubilant organist said: 'a thumping good popular choir. I'd have never kept them together and so enthusiastic if I'd expected them to learn how to read music.'

7

An Invaluable Guide to Vicars

During my choirboy days our vicar was a revered, rather distant figure. We knew little about him except that he was a person very much in charge. At church, he had a separate vestry and would only appear in the choir vestry for the choir prayer immediately before a service. He would smile – a remote smile, I always felt – perhaps have a brief word with one or two of us and we would address him as 'Sir'. I sometimes wondered if he knew any of our names, but I think that was the job of the junior curate who kept in touch with our families.

Towards the end of my term as a treble singer when my voice was about to break and I'd be drafted into the 'back row' with the men to see how my adult voice would develop, the whole vicar situation changed. I learned from choir friends in the same transitional position in other parishes that all vicars were not the same. There was evidence to show that there was a wide variety ranging from the delightful to the impossible, and we compiled a dossier using some imagination and, we hoped, a sense of humour that would be tolerated now that we were adults.

Dynamic progressive vicars are on the increase these days. They are easy to spot – in fact, you can't miss them. They are generally elephantine characters who blunder into parishes and make a clean sweep. That is, they alter everything that has been done before – whether it's for better or worse.

They are also very keen on calling together the whole congregation for innumerable discussions. These discussions are to persuade the congregation to believe that they have a say in the running of the church, and to enable the vicar to ram home his own views on everything and condemn everybody with differing views as stick-in-the-muds, reactionaries or downright enemies of the Church.

Such fearless words rather upset a lot of the less intelligent members of the congregation, who don't seem to understand about the Divine Right of Vicars, or that the vicar always knows best. They therefore go off to other churches and take their children away from the Sunday School, or join the Labour Party. But the vicar still keeps on saying and doing Dynamic, Progressive things, and in due course he is noticed by the Bishop, who soon hustles him off to a nice job in a cathedral or a fashionable church. And from then on he settles down happily, leaves things exactly as they are, and is never any further trouble to anyone.

Musical vicars are often not very musical at all.

But the less they know about music the more they strive to create the impression that they are experts, and they take a great deal of trouble in finding out what they are supposed to like and dislike, to be in the prevailing musical fashion.

Thus, they feel it their Christian and artistic duty firmly to suppress all popular hymns that happen to be Victorian, and if there are any which are so popular that they can't be suppressed without emptying the church, they introduce new tunes for them which the congregation have never heard of, and don't like when they do hear them. These are known as simpler, more beautiful, tunes.

Despite the vicar's efforts at enlightenment there is, however, always someone who dies and has instructed that a famous Victorian hymn, which is popular at football matches, shall be sung at their funeral. And with disappointment and sorrow the vicar allows this, bravely striving to keep the expression of pain from his face and discreetly withholding his own voice from the swelling and dreadful sound.

But musical vicars never give up. They are forever introducing wonderful opportunities for their flocks to educate themselves in the appreciation of modern church music. Recitals of modern organ music, for instance, are particularly encouraged. It is always such a pity when a musical vicar finds, as he so often seems to, that he cannot attend such recitals himself, owing to so many other pressing parish commitments. Musical vicars are very unselfish.

The Man's Man vicar uses many devices to show he is a Man's Man. One of the most popular is to burst into a pub and barge straight into the middle of a group of men who are quietly relaxing over a pint at the end of the day. The idea is to start a cheery chat among them about the Things that Really Matter, but quite often the men don't seem in the mood for cheery chats about anything. They just want to sit there. After a time, however, they can generally be pushed into a few well-worn excuses to explain why they don't come to church and the Man's Man vicar immediately agrees with them when they say about why they never darken the church door. He also makes some killingly funny remarks about his 'dog collar' and wears it as little as possible, preferring to perpetuate his image in a loud check shirt and even louder check tie. You can see he is a Man's Man all right.

His sermons are down-to-earth, straight-from-the-shoulder, man-to-man talks. Even the elderly ladies who comprise most of his congregation enjoy them in a shocked kind of way.

Artistic vicars often suffer a great deal, particularly when they take over new parishes and find the church full of dreadful Victorian stained-glass windows representing saints with dinner-plate halos and long red and blue garments that look like nightshirts.

Artistic vicars always try to persuade the church council to remove Victorian stained-glass windows, but as most church councils don't seem to know or care anything about art, and as the windows are generally memorials to very important Indian Army officers and local tradesmen, it's very difficult to do anything about them, and the artistic vicar has to go on suffering.

Then, of course, there are the heavyweight brass lecterns. Artistic vicars often don't like these; they like simple, beautiful wooden ones. But there is always someone who has polished and cherished the brass lectern for 40 years and refuses to give up the job, so the vicar is again frustrated.

There are many other things in the church which the artistic vicars *could* worry about, such as lethal electric-light systems and defunct heating systems, but lighting and heating systems never seem very beautiful whether they work or not, so artistic vicars don't worry about them.

There is just a slim chance that an artistic vicar will find a fellow spirit in his parish and then he does feel a little happier and finds that he can endure the surrounding Philistines with a slightly more cheerful and forgiving spirit. But in most cases he is on his own, and he eventually moves on to another parish, a disappointed and still suffering man.

And in the new parish he generally finds that he's jumped from the frying pan into the fire. He probably comes up against an organist who does barbaric things like churning out very loud versions of Wagner grand marches at the conclusion of a service in which he (the vicar) had been trying to fill the minds of the congregation with beautiful serene thoughts.

Artistic vicars *really do* suffer a great deal.

Trying vicars try to agree with all the usual warring factions in the parish and they end up being very trying to everyone. Trying vicars readily agree with the youth club leader that it is the church's duty to provide a bigger hall and more equipment for the healthy, high-spirited, misunderstood members of the youth club, and they agree just as whole-heartedly with the church council that the way to ward off a further spate of broken windows, smashed billiard tables and apoplectic neighbours is to close down the youth club altogether. When cornered by the advanced young organist they are all in favour of his demand that the Philistine congregation should no longer be allowed to wallow in the debased sentimentality of Victorian hymn tunes, and when ambushed at the back of the church by the said Philistines they vehemently declare that somebody's ghastly new apology for a tune for 'Lead, kindly Light' is an insult to Cardinal Newman.

The snag occurs when all the belligerents clash head-on at the church council meeting, and all appeal to the vicar for support. He is then very good at making long soothing speeches in which he says absolutely nothing at all and smiles at every scowling face in turn. He then concludes by flashing a kind of all-embracing communal smile which is meant to unite the whole council in charity and goodwill, and says that if everybody would just spare a little consideration for their neighbour and all would act in the Christian spirit of give and take, their small – and let's face it, friends – very unimportant difficulties would soon be entirely resolved. The church council who have not the slightest intention of sparing considerations or giving in to each other in any way, and who cherish their difficulties as the most precious part of their church life, receive this with a blank silence, which the vicar takes as a heartening sign of deep and serious meditation. The meeting over, the members split up into their well-defined opposition groups and stand about all over the place arguing, and the trying vicar passes homeward through their midst confident that *this* time everything will be all right.

Public spirited vicars are not often seen in church. They are too busy getting themselves elected on to town committees and into local papers. ('Vicar hits out at antiquated sewerage works – "Public disgrace. Does the Council really *care*?"')

It is absolutely essential that this type of vicar possesses two great advantages. He must have a powerful, dominating presence so that the town dignitaries notice that he's there, and don't doze off while he is upbraiding them about the local public disgraces. And he must possess a really dedicated curate who can visit and soothe all the common-or-garden members of the congregation who keep on making rude, uneducated remarks about such things as not receiving a visit from the vicar since grandfather's funeral on August Monday of one year to Our Daphne's wedding bonanza on Easter Monday two years later.

Public spirited vicars are, of course, very keen on their flock's being public spirited also, with the result that half the congregation find themselves members of every conceivable organization in the town, and the other half form a sort of opposition group and remain in a perpetual state of inactivity and disgrace.

8

Still Untouched by Time's Rude Hand

It is still one of the most attractive beautiful village churches that I know. It is tucked away in a West Country backwater, quite unsuspected by the hordes of visitors who come to admire the great cathedral a few miles away. To those travellers who do chance upon it, the retired schoolmistress who acts as its verger describes it as an early eighteenth-century gem: all of a period, always lovingly cared for, its structure never 'restored' or altered in any way by arrogant architect or bodging builder. Over nearly 200 years all renovation and redecoration has kept faithfully to the original conception. Wondrously, it stands today much as it must have originally appeared – a gem of a building indeed.

But there is a skeleton in the cupboard – in the choir vestry to be exact. The most original part of the church must surely be the choir vestry, for as far as anyone can discover it has never been renovated or redecorated or attended to at all. Each time the hands of experts have been reverently applied to keep the jewel in pristine condition the choir vestry has been quietly ignored. The verger, lecturing occasional visitors, keeps them well away from the choir vestry, and no one else connected with the church ever goes near it – except, of course, the choir, for whom it is a sort of spiritual home.

The story goes that during the church's early years the then rector and church council quarrelled with the choir over the frequent use of some particularly crude versions of some of the psalms. The choir, who were especially drawn to these particular versions, refused in solid peasant fashion to stop singing them and so were more or less banished to the choir vestry, from whence they emerged defiant Sunday by Sunday to bawl the psalms ever more crudely.

In nature's good time both the choir and the crude psalms passed on, but the tradition had taken root that, because if its dreadful associations, the choir vestry was not the kind of place that any self-respecting member of the parish should have anything to do with. Until very recently, although the present choir were accepted as a sort of inevitable, entrenched nuisance, the choir vestry remained a largely out-of-bounds, out-of-mind append-age to the jewel that was the church.

And this whole situation suited the present choir admir-ably. In the outlawed choir vestry they regularly practised unhindered the hymns and anthems that the rector – like his early eighteenth-century forebear – couldn't stand, and here they decided which edicts from the rector and the church council they would oppose and which they would simply ignore. The independent spirit of the early choir lived on in their stronghold, and in the great majority of cases the choir ignored the edicts rather than opposed them, thereby saving no end of time attending special democratic discussions which the rector and the church council arranged to impose their views firmly on all who didn't agree with them.

As a friend of one or two members of the choir, who occasionally joins them when I am in the vicinity, I am happily familiar with the companionable chaos of the choir vestry. It is cocooned in a comfortable, safe atmosphere – a feeling of being quite untouched by the machinations of dynamic, new-thinking rectors and stick-in-the-mud church councils. Its physical features enhance its unique atmosphere. As will be appreciated, it is quite impossible to detect the original colour of the walls. In any case they are now much covered by dozens of faded pictures and photographs of the choir through the ages, supported by historic, framed, yellowed local-newspaper cuttings about members getting married, having babies and getting buried, or going off to war, or being transported for poaching or rioting, and setting fire to haystacks.

In the centre of the room a huge, battered, basic farmhouse table is always littered with piles of anthems as yellowed as the newspaper cuttings, and a miscellany of empty drink cans, a huge grimy aspidistra called George and a pile of pre-Second World War choir registers full of spidery writing and interestingly shaped blots. Along the entire length of one wall leans a spare church pew that doesn't look very comfortable, although you can't sit on it anyway as it provides accommodation for a tangled mass of rusty black cassocks and off-white surplices, veteran hymn books and psalters, various tarnished candlesticks and a broken hymn board. There being few other seating possibilities, the choir members sit about on the table or lean on a monster iron heating-stove of great antiquity which, rumour has it, has never been successfully ignited.

The whole remarkable scene is lighted by three narrow gothic windows, covered on the outside by a splendid weave of uninhibited ivy, and on the inside by the undisturbed dust of ages.

Early on Sunday mornings the organist, a character who looks uncannily like the popular conception of Sherlock Holmes, is always at the ill-treated table, engaged in his traditional pastime of doctoring the rector's hymn list for the coming service by identifying all the new tunes the rector has indicated and deleting them in favour of the 'old favourites' that the choir always sing. 'There!' he pronounced in satisfied tones one morning after I'd been assisting him. 'That's better – that's fine.'

'Doesn't the rector ever realize that the choir never sing the tunes he chooses?' I asked, puzzled.

'Oh, he realizes all right,' he assured me. 'Oh, he knows how we feel. He understands, he just trusts that, if he keeps on long enough, one of these days we may give in and sing what he wants.'

'He seems a very trusting man,' I said.

'Yes, he is,' agreed the organist. 'We do appreciate that and in return we're reasonable. We always sing his tunes on the Sunday nearest his birthday or if we don't know the old tune anyway.'

'That's nice,' I enthused.

'Yes, we generally get on with him well enough,' he admitted comfortably, 'just so long as he leaves us alone.'

And there seemed no civilized reason why the situation should not have continued happily unchanged in the twenty-first century – until the main nave roof suddenly, shockingly, let everything down. During the night of a particularly violent and unusual summer storm, the power of the wind and torrential rain was so great that it revealed a hitherto undetected weakness in some roof timbers, with the result that the nave of the church was flooded and a considerable portion of the exquisite painted ceiling showered the pews. In no time the main building was swathed in a tarpaulin and enmeshed in scaffolding, and the question arose urgently, 'Where shall we hold the services now?' There was no church hall, the vicarage was too small and an adjacent long-disused stable block had recently been reoccupied by a team of champion Shire show horses, who were attracting lots of visitors and increasing the weekend takings at the village pub most encouragingly. Eyes turned in horror to the choir vestry.

On the Friday evening a few days after the fatal storm, the choir were visited in their vestry by a sort of deputation from the church council, led by the rector. It was the first time that most of the party had ever seen inside the place and they stepped gingerly, cautiously, through the doorway and hesitated, bunching together like travellers in a mythical land of horror who had suddenly come upon the lair of some hideous giant reptile. The choir were practising one of their favourite warlike Victorian hymns all about Christian soldiers being victorious and slaying the unrighteous left, right and centre, and the deputation had to wait till they'd roared through every one of the numerous verses before the unnerving sound abated and the deputation could draw near. Then the rector forced a ghastly smile and said how splendid it all sounded. And while his colleagues peered around unbelievingly in the failing grey light from the ivy-choked windows the rector enthused to the choir on how fortunate and grateful the whole parish felt that they had a worthy building at hand where services could continue while the main church was being repaired. The members of the church council backed him up with frozen smiles and untranslatable mutterings, and the rector went on to declare that really all that was needed was a little reorganization of the place so that some rows of chairs could be accommodated. 'We'll have everything going ahead in no time,' he forecast, trying hard to hold the all-embracing team-spirit that he used at church council meetings when everyone had just voted down his latest brainwave for revitalizing the Family Service.

'We can move this very large table out of the way,' he continued quickly, taking advantage of the shocked silence from the choir. 'It is very big and will make room for quite a lot of chairs.' The organist bent to retrieve a fallen pile of anthems that had been toppled by a nervous and rather clumsy member of the invading party. 'You can't,' he said. The rector regarded him brightly, encouragingly, 'Er, can't what?' he asked. 'You can't move the table,' explained Sherlock. 'It was put together inside this vestry. It's too big to go out through the door. It's meant to stay here.'

'Ah! Part of the building. Wonderful! Wonderful!' chuckled the rector, now becoming jocular as well as bright and encouraging. 'Yes, indeed, part of the building, just like our wonderful choir! We could take it apart and shove the bits into the churchyard – the table, I mean, not the choir!' His chuckle became a guffaw.

The guffaw died abruptly in the stunned silence of both choir and church council. Since the days of crude psalms the choir and the church council had wholeheartedly disagreed with each other, and thoroughly understood each other, and everything had worked well. The rector had understood nothing of this wisdom of the ages and blundered in where angels feared to tread. Some members of the church council had been mildly interested in being vouchsafed a sight of the interior of the choir vestry, but enough was enough. You meddled with tradition at your peril. You revered tradition. It was a safe, sure foundation. The rector would have to listen and learn.

From a nephew who ran an outside catering business, the organist obtained the free loan of a large heated tent that fitted into an unoccupied part of the churchyard and accommodated the services very well. In seven months the church had been expertly restored to its former perfection – except, of course, the choir vestry, where tradition was rigidly respected. So everyone is happy.

There is a rumour that the rector, in these lean times for the Church, is considering opening the choir vestry as it stands as a museum, offering admittance at a small charge. But it is only a rumour that could one day provide yet another story to add to the records of priestly follies and failures.

9

No Latin, More Lumber

In the rural West Country town where my old maths
master many years ago gratefully retired and joined the
parish church choir, the neighbouring church of St John
has gradually taken over in importance from the parish
church. Nowadays, if the bishop or local MP or the town
council have occasion to attend a special church service, they always go to St John's. And if you want to be
married – or buried – in style, the thing to do is to go to
St John's.

St John's has a lot in its favour. It was designed by an
eminent and most expensive Victorian architect who
lavished on it a splendour that no twenty-first-century
criticism can dim, and complemented it at a respect-
ful distance by delightful villas and gardens. Later years
bestowed on it some of the finest modern stained-glass
windows for miles. It also possesses a superb organ and
boasts a choir that repeatedly wins top awards at the most
prestigious music festivals and keeps on getting invited
to sing on television. Things are different with the parish
church. It is approached down an alley with a gas lamp
that never works, and is flanked by two boarded-up ware-
houses and a very suspicious-looking pub. The parish
church is so old that no one knows who designed it or if it
was designed at all. Over the centuries local jobbing build-

ers have added bits here and there and pulled down other bits, and at the end of the eighteenth century the local landowner, who possessed untold wealth and no artistic taste whatsoever, built a monstrous family memorial chapel on to, and partly into, the side of the lady chapel – which explains the curiously lopsided appearance that the church presents today and the fact that the lady chapel has three bricked-up gothic windows, a door that can't be opened and a flamboyant, two-ton, black marble memorial, whose inscription and fat guardian cherub seem to have half disappeared into a wall.

In the 1870s the harmonium was replaced with a large strident organ. This was placed in the remains of the lady chapel and was used by the organ builder as a demonstration model to impress prospective customers. Consequently all kinds of extra pipes were added and the one surviving chapel window completely blocked up, producing a sort of twilight zone where the ladies of the present choir robe, they being a comparatively new addition to the choir and not being accommodated in the still all-male preserve of the choir vestry.

The main body of the church is bright and cheerful. A number of large pillars of various shapes and periods stand about in the nave, some supporting arches and others now supporting nothing in particular. These might prove rather disconcerting to a stranger, who could find that wherever he sat he couldn't see the preacher. The regulars, however, have long discovered good vantage points where they can see the preacher even if he can't see them – which gives the congregation a feeling of privacy, with the opportunity of a quiet doze if the sermon proves to be a repeat or not to their liking.

On each side of the nave there are short flights of little stone steps which lead up to nowhere save a small indentation in the wall, and these are always covered with vases of flowers and potted plants and coloured drawings by the Sunday School children of people like St Paul and the vicar and the school dinner lady. In the main aisle are large metal grilles that act as warm-air vents and also trap people with high heels and blow out gales of icy air in mid-winter when the boiler usually breaks down.

The choir has been almost completely hidden from the congregation since the end of the sixteenth century, when the fort-like stone chancel screen was erected; but they sing so lustily that they are always well and truly heard, if not seen, and this circumstance helps the organist considerably when he finds it necessary to reprimand the choirboys during the service. After all, it is rather embarrassing if you have to drag a wrongdoer from the choir stalls by the scruff of his neck and hurl him into the vestry in full view of the congregation.

Things have been pottering along happily at the parish church for a long time now. Over the years, during visits to my old maths master, I have become an accepted member of the choir and I can't recall anything ever changing.

But recently something started to happen.

'When you come up here this time,' wrote my friend in a letter completing arrangements for a holiday I was about to spend with him, 'prepare yourself for a shock. You'll be amazed at the size of the congregation at the parish church. It's nearly trebled in the past six months. The congregation of St John's have been coming over to us in droves! I'll tell you all about it when I see you.'

I was intrigued. Why on earth were the congregation of St John's coming to the parish church? An outrageous thought struck me. Could it be that for some mad, mad reason they suddenly preferred the parish church choir to their own superb choir. It was a very large, jolly, do-it-yourself choir – indeed, it outnumbered the congregation – and everyone sang so heartily and at such volume that, even if you didn't know a note of a particular item, you were not afraid of having a go, because a wrong note or two didn't make much difference as long as everyone ended up more or less together.

But they were different at St John's. What had happened there? Over lunch on the day of my arrival, my old master made things clear. As is so often the case, the trouble had started with a new vicar. Apparently, within days of his induction he had told the church council that a church building, however splendid, was not a monument of a place reserved for set services on Sundays for a minority who liked that kind of thing. It must be a place full of vigorous life where things went on all the time, 'a here and now place', open to all with a great welcome.

And in no time at all the great big welcome had taken shape and St John's had been transformed into one of those churches where the noticeboards are completely covered by posters announcing all kinds of goings-on in the church from jazz concerts and keep-fit demonstrations to exhibitions of modern art, political dialogues and protest meetings about filthy pavements and cars parked in the cemetery, and where it is well-nigh impossible for a stranger to discover when, or if, any actual church services take place.

And St John's had turned into one of the great, big

welcome churches with a vengeance. My old master reckoned that when you turned up for choral Matins on Sunday these days you were just as likely to find yourself watching a performance by the local junior ballet company and, as for Evensong, you'd probably be confronted with a crew putting up a set for *The Pirates of Penzance.*

Things are so much more reliable at the parish church. You know what you're getting. The blue gothic noticeboard displays plainly, in gold lettering, a full list of the services over the name of the vicar who left the parish five years ago. My old master says that they'll have to get around to putting the new man's name there one of these days. Although, after all, as he points out, a vicar is a vicar and the one on the noticeboard and the present one are almost identical anyway. They are both from the same Oxford college, both are ardent champions of *Hymns A & M* (all editions), both have large wives who ride small horses and make tons of jam each year in aid of organ funds and local operatic societies, both can't sing a note in tune, and both believe in good solid half-hour sermons.

And it seemed that out-of-date noticeboards advertising vicars who weren't there troubled the erstwhile congregation of St John's not at all. As the new vicar of St John's rejoiced at rising audience figures with the introduction of every new attraction, the congregation-count continued to plummet as members flocked to the parish church.

The whole situation was, of course, a bit embarrassing for the regulars at the parish church. For one thing, they had a job finding enough hymn books. Indeed, the vicar's warden had to dust off a whole bookshelf of them that hadn't been used for years and were covered with damp spots and, as the migration continued, he was forced to disinter the less disreputable ones from those that had been retired to the back of the broom cupboard since the days of the last-but-one vicar.

Then there was the vexed question of the side aisle. The side aisle, never in living memory having had any occupants, had long been the repository for all the lumber that the verger couldn't hide in the broom cupboard, or the choir vestry. But now the new flock were already complaining about having to sit in a desert of dust surrounded by broken ladders, discarded bunting and old cement buckets, and the church warden had had to take action about the side aisle even before it could be discussed by the parochial church council, who always discussed everything at great length before doing nothing about it.

On the first Sunday of my visit to my old master, we arrived at the main door of the church where a considerable mass of people were trying to get in. Being members of the choir we could, of course, have avoided the crush by entering by the perfectly accessible choir vestry door, but the parish church is a very traditional church and one of its best-loved traditions is that the choir members always enter by the main door so that they can stand around at the back of the church gossiping with the congregation until precisely three minutes before the service is due to start. Then they all clatter up the main aisle to the vestry in the manner of would-be passengers chasing a departing train.

Just inside the door stood the verger, a dignified figure in a rusty black cassock splattered with candle-grease, who had been very put out by having his side-aisle domain upset by, as he put it, 'All there people who don't belong here.' He stared fixedly ahead, repeating, 'Mind the ladders, mind the ladders,' in the forbidding 'mind the gap' monotone of the public-address system at railway stations.

The warning was indeed timely because we were immediately confronted by a tottering barrier of rejected builders' materials and garden fête remains that the verger had removed from the side aisle without any clear idea of where to stow it.

The refugees from St John's were clambering over the obstruction valiantly and dusting themselves down. Some already seated in the side aisle were examining their kneelers – frail Victorian relics hastily rescued from the back of the coke shed – or finding the first hymn books. Others appeared to be engrossed in reading the inscriptions on the brass plates that are crammed on to every square inch of the walls. They recount the exploits of former militant members of the congregation who got caught up in the Crimean and Boer wars and, according to my old master, came home with greatly enhanced importance and made nuisances of themselves on the parochial church council and in the choir for years and years.

Meanwhile, the regulation three-minute period having arrived in which the choir had to get from the back of the church and, robed, into the chancel, we all took to our heels and, true to tradition, processed into the choir stalls dead on time.

I found myself sitting next to a knowing-looking youth who, on the occasion of my last visit, was still a treble, sitting in the front stall. During the reading of the first lesson he informed me in a loud croak that his voice had now broken and the choirmaster had put him in the back row with the men and told him to sing alto until his voice settled down to tenor or bass or something that was not too shattering. The choirmaster had said that he hoped he wouldn't turn out actually to be an alto because most parish church altos were shattering even in choirs that sang as lustily as theirs. You simply couldn't drown shattering altos. The knowing youth croaked appeasingly that he realized I was an alto, of course, but I wasn't shattering because I always sang tenor when we came to the really high bits. I said that was all right then, and tried to dissuade him from croaking at me for a bit by pretending to read one of the large brass memorial plates over the choir stalls opposite. But the youth had more to tell me. During the second lesson he handed me a copy of the anthem, Elvey's 'Arise, shine'. 'If we were in St John's choir,' he said, 'we'd probably be singing this in Latin. They're always doing Latin things there. What I say is, it's hard enough learning some of these things in English, let alone Latin.' He nodded vigorously. 'That'll be the next thing. You'll see. If their choir at St John's get fed up like their congregation, they'll be coming here and joining our choir and wanting to do all these Latin things.'

But my knowing friend was wrong. Not a single member of St John's choir applied to join the parish church choir. Not even the doings of the new showman-vicar could work that miracle. Our choir remains safe from the Latin influence. And in a roundabout way, our choir proved to be the champion of St John's congregation and choir in their darkest hour. Driven to desperation by the unholy prospect of singing with the parish church choir and organ, the St John's choir forced a last-ditch confrontation with the new vicar and reached a compromise whereby full importance would be given to the services where the choir sang such beautiful Latin settings and anthems. In return, the choir would put some stuffing into the vicar's recently formed contemporary music group, which was supposed to be spearheading his new lunch-time concerts and wasn't having much success to date owing to its only having three members. The vicar had even offered to advertise the service times on a new fluorescent poster on the main noticeboard.

The parish church people were glad that everything had been resolved so amicably. The verger was particularly pleased. He was able to make a completely new start with his lumber and stack it back in the side aisle far more tidily than had been possible after years of random stacking. In fact, when he had finished his task, he was overjoyed to find that he'd left himself a great deal more room for a great deal more lumber. The future looked fine. As my old maths master summed up: 'No Latin, more lumber.' Everyone was happy.

10

The Traditionalists

Edward (never Ted – he always wore a suit and tie), a school friend whom I'd lost touch with since late school-days, came across one of my 'Choir Story' books recently and felt I'd be interested in some details of what goes on at his church in a lovely village in southern England to where he retired some years ago. While he's been a regular churchgoer, Edward has never aspired to being a chorister, boy or man. He sings as a member of the congregation, of course, but not too loudly as the sound tends to result in startled or indignant glances from new or visiting members of the congregation.

Edward's church is an original eighteenth-century building, flamboyantly enlarged by the Victorians and disastrously disguised in the twentieth century by the blatant installation in the side chapel of a 'tea-and-gossip' bar for use after the Sunday morning family service. Edward says that the bar is a very popular feature, in fact he reckons that more people congregate for the tea and gossip section than actually attend the service.

The nave of the church has three aisles which, by pop-ular usage, have rounded up the congregation into three groups. The left-hand aisle is the preserve of young fami-lies with children, where the wall monuments are mostly obliterated with sticky-taped pictures of the Sunday school children's ideas of dinosaurs, parents, St Paul, the vicar, the vicar's cat and the local postman who rides a tricycle with solid tyres.

Throughout this left-hand aisle, for a full half-hour until the last moments before the Sunday morning service begins, the jolly sound of enthusiastic greetings by parents struggling above that of the no less enthusiastic hub-hub from offspring with skates and scooters, makes the whole aisle resemble rush hour at a main line railway station – until the organist decides it's about time things got moving in the right direction and drowns everything with something like 'The Grand March' from *Aida* at full blast.

Halfway through the service, the atmosphere becomes a little quieter – it is realized that the children would not want to sit through the sermon so they are led off to draw more pictures in the village hall next door and – to quote Edward – 'a frighteningly tall lady called Miss Ermintrude with a ramrod-like figure and wildly flowing blonde hair, out of a bottle, stands guard at the church door to make sure that only children leave, and not anybody else who also wouldn't want to hear the sermon. Nobody gets away with any kind of backsliding when Miss Ermintrude is around.'

Now, the middle aisle of the church is entirely different. Miss Ermintrude belongs to the group that sits there; in fact she is the ring-leader. The vicar, a middle-aged family man with the necessary sense of humour for the job, is very careful in dealing with this lot. He refers to them respectfully as 'mature', never 'old' or, like some exasperated colleagues, 'old nuisances', for these are the members who really run the parish with a large majority on the parochial church council, whose main aim is to make sure that the vicar doesn't push through his cherished idea of ripping out all the church pews and filling the place with orange plastic chairs for the sake of Christian togetherness.

These middle aisle lot are indeed different from the crowd in the first aisle. They are all very regular at services and turn up serene and confident and well on time. Within the church they nod politely to each other, speak in low tones and respectfully listen to all the vicar has to say about Christian togetherness and joy and giving more money to save the sagging vicarage roof and replace the defunct church boiler. Then they all shake hands with him and say kind things about the sermon and disappear till next Sunday, not even glancing at the 'tea and gossip' bar merrymakers as they pass.

Edward points out that the right-hand (third) aisle of the church is interesting because on the walls you can still view the work of a considerable nineteenth-century sculptor that is not sticky-taped over 'with juvenile art efforts of dinosaurs and vicars and things'. He says there is a trio of military memorials and one to a well-loved and respected eighteenth-century parson who turned out to be a highwayman in his spare time and paid for the church's first organ.

This right-hand aisle is reserved exclusively for the regular latecomers to the Sunday morning service. They are worshippers from a neighbouring village where the church closed ages ago, who don't use cars and are conditioned to relying on the three-hourly bus service on Sundays. And the bus company arranges for the Sunday morning bus to arrive just ten minutes after the service begins. Edward says there is a convenient side entrance for the right-hand aisle so that latecomers don't disturb the children who are disturbing the rest of the congregation.

As Edward finished his tale of the three aisles an intriguing thought now struck me. 'What about the choir?' I asked. 'How do they fit into the jig-saw?'

Edward considered briefly. 'I suppose they don't really. They *annoy* people of course – well, all choirs annoy somebody, don't they. The young family-people in the left-hand aisle get annoyed with the organist and choir for making more singing noise than they do during the service. And in the middle aisle there's Miss Ermintrude and her confederates – they don't like the choir very much. They don't like the way the choir carry on. Miss Ermintrude says it's not nice y'see, they hold choir practice in the back room of the Lamb and Flag instead of the vestry and that's not nice at all. She says they've got a position to uphold and that's not the bar at the Lamb and Flag. She's the editor of the parish magazine and, in the most lady-like manner, she has explained to the vicar that she cannot include reference to choir practice in the diary as, try as she may, she cannot acknowledge that the goings-on at the Lamb and Flag are serious choir practices. She says she regards them as merely a crowd of rather coarse people having a rowdy sing-song in a pub.'

My thoughts returned to the vicar with the sense of humour. 'What a hero!' I exclaimed – 'Or at least what a clever stage manager! How,' I asked, 'does he not only hold this parish together, but also continue to make a success of such an odd assortment. What's his secret?'

Edward grinned. 'No secret. It's the choir.'

I must have sounded bemused. 'The choir!' I echoed. 'But they *annoy* people.'

Edward agreed. 'Oh yes, they do that all right. They are also *traditionalists*. We've had the same sort of choir here for 150 years – they sing the same Victorian anthems and settings, the same tunes to the hymns, use the same back room at the Lamb and Flag for choir practice and won't even take a step into the present and call hymns "praise songs".'

'And so?' I prompted. 'And so,' he repeated comfortably, 'whether we like it or not, just below the would-be trendy modern surface of this parish, traditionalism is alive and well and stops us throwing out everything that was *good* in the past.'

Edward chuckled. 'Mind you, that lot in the choir have no idea that they are doing the parish a service – they just like bawling Victorian hymns in the Lamb and Flag on Friday nights!'

Edward continued to beam. 'And, of course, there is one of the premier annual events. We have the oh, so traditional Choir Benefit Evensong in aid of the senior choir's summer outing and dinner to show the congregation's appreciation of all the joy the choir gives them throughout the year.' (According to Miss Ermintrude, a notorious occasion involving crates of beer in the back of the coach.)

Everybody in the parish turns up for the Choir Benefit Evensong, including the brewery brass band. The three-aisle plan goes overboard and people grab seats wherever they can. This is a heart-warming occasion when the church is packed to the roof and the vicar welcomes everyone to 'this wonderful demonstration of parish togetherness' and declares 'our great love and admiration for the choir', reading from the same tattered folder that he's used for years. Everybody puts lots of money into the collection plate and steels themselves for two non-stop hours of the choir charging through the same swashbuckling Victorian church music that they've performed for years. Some of the congregation know it so well they whistle along with the catchier bits. Then, as one particularly riotous chorus reaches its climax, the whole congregation rises to an overwhelming standing ovation – well, not quite overwhelming, in case this would encourage the choir to carry on regardless and delay the fabulous celebratory supper at the vicarage which everyone has specially come for and which, the vicar knows with confidence, will unite the people of the three-aisle congregation for another happy year.

11

The Choir's Fashion Problem

For a considerable time everything had been going right in the parish. By some extraordinary fluke, the vicar had been choosing hymns for services that everybody liked, no one had complained about the choirboys chewing sweets throughout Evensong, not a single child had been thrown out of the Sunday school for vandalism, and the only man who understood the workings of the evil-tempered church boiler had not made his usual monthly threat to resign. Even the members of the church council had been agreeing with each other.

The vicar felt completely out of her depth, and absolutely unprepared to deal with the situation. Not only had she received no complaints and encountered no opposition from anyone, but last Sunday a woman who had sat in the pew under the pulpit every Matins for 25 years, and never failed to attack every sermon she'd ever heard, had actually rung the vicar to say how much comfort and joy she had received from her latest offering.

The whole thing was getting quite out of hand.

And then, like a sandstorm in the desert, there arose the case of the new choir cassocks.

I had been a guest in the choir of the frowning, grime-veiled London church on a number of occasions, and when I entered the vestry on this, my latest visit, I sensed immediately that something more than the usual unholy uproar was afoot.

A gigantic, drooping-moustached gentleman, who usually bellowed bass down the back of my neck and always seemed to be passing a bag of Liquorice Allsorts up and down the choir stalls during the sermon, rolled across to me, his usually beaming face now purple with anger. He was accompanied by his constant companion, a small red-haired tenor called Fred. Both were arrayed in new single-breasted black cassocks which, not being buttoned up, flapped aimlessly around them.

'What about these?' the gigantic bass appealed to me. 'There's a new man in the congregation – only been here about five years – who thinks we should have new cassocks, so he sees the vicar and goes out and buys 'em, just like that.'

'Just like that,' echoed Fred.

'We're going to call a choir committee meeting about this, pretty sharp,' thundered the gigantic bass. 'The choir weren't even consulted.'

'That's right,' agreed Fred, eagerly, 'not even *consulted.*'

'We don't like the colour, for a start,' pursued the gigantic bass, cornering me between a broken iron heating-stove and a disreputable-looking piano. 'We've *never* had black cassocks here.'

'Always been a green-blue,' explained Fred, gazing morosely at his new garment. 'Rather unusual, really. I think that when we first had 'em they were supposed to be just blue. I think . . .'

His companion drowned him. 'The vicar's not getting away with this – committee meeting at my place, just after Matins.'

'Single-breasted, too,' said Fred. 'Imagine how long it'll take to do up all those little buttons. We'll have to come earlier.'

'The vicar will have to wait,' amended the gigantic bass. 'When she's done up the three buttons on her double-breasted cassock she'll have to wait while we do up the 15 on our single-breasted ones.'

Four or five more choirmen had now arrived and were standing aghast before their cassock pegs, on each of which hung a brand-new cassock.

'What's the meaning of this? Where's my cassock?' exploded one gentleman, who was carrying a copy of Mendelssohn's *Elijah* and the *News of the World*.

'New cassocks. Someone's bought 'em. We've got to wear 'em,' explained Fred.

The questioner reverently placed his *News of the World* across two pegs and flung 'Elijah' on top of a cupboard. 'I don't know what we're coming to.'

'The trouble is, we're not appreciated,' said the gigantic bass. 'They don't understand a good choir here. Pearls before swine. First the vicar stops us during anthems because she says they're too long . . .'

'It was the 20-minute one the other Sunday that did it,' put in Fred.

'. . . then the church council cuts the beer money for the annual outing, and now' – the gigantic bass's mind seemed to boggle at the unparalleled insult – 'we've got to wear new cassocks.'

'Black ones, too,' said Fred, 'with all those little buttons down the front.'

We stood, a suddenly stunned circle, contemplating a future blighted by the torture of the little black buttons.

The door leading from the church swung open vigorously and two men entered, one giving the unmistakable impression of driving the other. The driven one was a small nervous-looking type, who appeared to be searching desperately for a way of escape. The driver was a lordly, expansive, pin-striped gentleman whom I knew to be the vicar's warden. His great joy in life was to collar visitors the moment they ventured inside the church door, announce with quiet dignity who he was, and firmly hustle them into a conducted tour of the building. Indeed, he had devoted a great deal of his time for many years to hammering home his wildly inaccurate history of the church, and was considered a great authority.

The reluctant gentleman was obviously a visitor, and the vicar's warden was just as obviously determined to show him everything in the church, even the choir. After explaining that the vestry was a later addition in the church (he waved his arms at the barn-like Victorian solidity and proclaimed rapturously 'Georgian, you see. Very fine,') he stood well back from us and said, 'And that's our choir.'

To show that, although tremendously lordly, he was also very friendly and willing to speak to just anyone, he remarked to the vestry at large, 'So you've got new cassocks then. Very nice, very nice. Good, good.' And when his words met with that curious lack of response with which so many of his words usually were met, his friendliness continued unabated, and he stood a little further back and said 'Splendid! Splendid!'

The effect was rather spoilt for him when the vestry door opened abruptly behind him and pushed him unceremoniously. A little old man, wearing a long, extremely dirty raincoat, and with his trouser bottoms tied round with bootlaces, entered the vestry and walked across to a cupboard, where he divested himself of the raincoat and put on a rusty black gown and an extremely crumpled and frayed university hood. He made no attempt to remove the bootlaces and took no notice whatsoever of the fuming choir who, in turn, took no notice whatsoever of him.

'And that's our organist,' said the vicar's warden.

The organist *never* took any notice of the choir. He didn't believe in choirs, especially this one. He just couldn't believe that the congregation couldn't sing without the choir. In fact he couldn't visualize *any* congregation's standing dumb when he was playing a hymn, because he knew that he played so well. All the choir did was to upset him right through the service by singing in front of the organ, or behind the organ, and then they upset him again after the service by kicking up such a din in the vestry that it quite spoilt his beautiful voluntary. He didn't like the choir at all.

He couldn't help hearing the down-to-earth remarks that rose from the group of choirmen around the cassock pegs. Again and again he caught the words 'Resign' and 'St Jude's would be pleased to have us' and 'What about the Methodists?' He smiled discreetly as he climbed into the organ loft. In his mind's eye he saw the choir stalls beautifully empty. He couldn't help feeling happy.

On leaving the vestry, the vicar's warden had driven his visitor into the Sunday school to show him what was going on there. A football match was, in fact, going on just then, and as the two passed a glass partition, the ball misguidedly found its way through the glass and on to the head of the visitor. The visitor said that it was quite all right and that he wasn't hurt, and scuttled thankfully away.

The vicar's warden, looking thunderous, investigated and found that the culprit was a sturdy urchin who had never treated him with anything like the proper respect when he had ordered him out of the vicar's pear trees, or out of the cupboard, at the end of the church, where one flick of a switch could plunge the whole place into darkness. He ordered the urchin out of the Sunday school there and then, and told him that a letter to his parents would be following very shortly. Two little girls who came into the classroom looked at him uncertainly. He smiled at them graciously. He felt very happy.

The vicar walked up the centre aisle of the church to the vestry. Everybody smiled at her. They all seemed so happy. Once again, not one member of the congregation had waylaid her in the porch with a complaint or a downright threat. She was becoming more and more disturbed.

She entered the vestry. Her expert eye took in the grim, accusing faces bunched together before her. The gigantic bass and Fred strode forward threateningly, their new unbuttoned cassocks flapping behind them like the wings of great birds of ill omen.

Then the vicar smiled her famous, winning smile and visibly relaxed. Like the organist and the vicar's warden, she felt happy. Things were getting back to normal.

12

Little Room for Change

It was one of those churches that crop up quite by chance when you are miles from anywhere in the middle of a day's rural walking. As I drew abreast of a lone, ragged group of villainously gnarled oak trees in a scrubby field, I became aware of a voice, uplifted and gravelly. 'They've always been the same,' it complained. 'Always!' A huge yard broom shot out from the trees into my path, scattering before it a confusion of empty beer cans, crisp bags, ice-cream cartons, dead flowers and a dirty handkerchief. An ancient wiry little man appeared on the other end of the broom. He didn't seem surprised at seeing me and continued to sweep up all over my feet, at the same time addressing me as if we were in familiar conversation. 'I've never known 'em to be any different,' he went on, 'and I've been verger here for 40 years; hooligans, all of 'em.'

'Who?' I asked.

'Why, the choir here of course,' he grated, thumbing back through the trees to what I now saw was a church – a sturdy, squat eighteenth-century pile flanked by a bunch of nonchalantly lolling gravestones and two huge shire horses who stood among them looking thoughtful. He came close to me and leaned on his broom. 'The women are as bad as the men,' he confided. 'Worse!'

'It happens,' I said.

He could see that I understood. 'Messy, slovenly, couldn't-care-less – that's the trouble with our choir lot,' he said. 'The choir vestry is always like a pigsty after Matins on Sundays. Mind you, it's only as big as a pigsty really so if you don't put things away and hang things up, and you leave your beer cans and things all over the place, it's quite a job to get through the doorway.'

'Beer cans?' I said.

'They always have some in for after Matins,' he explained. 'There's not a pub for miles.'

'Doesn't the vicar do anything about all this?' I asked. The verger looked puzzled. 'He never goes near the choir vestry,' he said. 'There's a dartboard in there and the darts fly straight across the doorway when the choir are having a game before the service – and the vicar's a little bit timid.'

'You mean he's reluctant to get mixed up with the darts flying across the doorway,' I said.

'Yes, he's timid in that way,' agreed the verger, and with a final flourish of the broom he swept the rubbish across the path into a ditch. 'Just come and have a look at what I'm talking about,' he invited, and led the way back through the churchyard, trailing the broom behind him so that when he reached the vestry doorway a considerable amount of debris was deposited back on the mat again. We stood there hemmed in by huge, heavy cupboards and a sort of table consisting of two massive boards resting on a pile of bricks and a little barrel by the side of which stood a bulging, cast-iron, Edwardian electric-fire with no elements. A tiny, cracked washbasin rested between two sagging brass rods from which drooped various venerable choir robes, and beside the one small window hung the aforementioned dartboard and a framed certificate that the choir had been awarded at a choir festival in 1906.

'What do they keep in these cupboards?' I asked, intrigued.

'Oh, there's nothing in them,' explained my guide. 'They're damp, y'see. Things go mildewed. The PCC are going to do something about them – well, they were going to five years ago when I was on the PCC. I'm not on it now – fed up with the arguing and late nights – but I think they're still going to do something.'

'Where's the music kept?' I asked.

He looked at me. 'Music? Oh, I don't think our choir has anything like that. There'd be no room for it in here anyway – enough rubbish as it is. No, the organist has got these tunes on bits of paper that he brings, and he takes 'em back again after the service.'

Suddenly there was a disturbance at the door and I was nudged further into the tiny space. Turning, I found myself looking into the eager, comical face of a magnificent Dalmatian dog. 'That's Berlioz,' introduced the verger – 'with the organist.' The organist, who brought up the rear, was as friendly as Berlioz and looked rather like him. He explained that he had just dropped in to practise something he'd not played for years. '"War March of the Priests" – Mendelssohn, you know,' he explained. 'This girl who's getting married here next Saturday wants it to come up the aisle with.' Doubtless he saw some surprise on my face. 'Well, it's more realistic than "Moonlight and Roses" in her case I suppose,' he said. 'She's a women's libber and keeps on threatening to become a priest.'

'How many have you in the choir?' I asked.

'Well, we can always depend on eight anyway – four men and four girls,' he said, 'and the vicar's sister joins us if we're singing anything like "Fight the good fight" or "Onward, Christian soldiers".'

I was puzzled. The three of us and Berlioz were already filling the vestry to overflowing. 'How do you all manage to robe here?' I asked. The organist looked around. 'Yes, it's a bit tight I suppose,' he conceded, 'but we're all very experienced – been here for years – and of course Berlioz doesn't normally come in here. He sits with me on the organ stool.'

The verger now noticed the untidy state of the doormat that he had inadvertently caused by trailing his broom, and with a deep sigh took himself off with the mat into the churchyard. The organist, flexing his fingers and making little cracking noises, invited me to come into the chancel to see the organ, and there we sat, all three of us on the organ stool while the organist ran through 'The War March of the Priests' from memory. It sounded all right to me but I don't think Berlioz was very impressed because he suddenly gave a single deep bark and regarded the organist with a look on his face like the one my old choirmaster used to direct to me when I messed up a simple treble solo and ruined the anthem.

'He's got a very good ear for music,' said the organist admiringly. 'The choir always know when they're not doing well on Sundays because he barks at the really bad spots.' He grinned. 'Sometimes he barks quite a lot, I can tell you. It keeps us on our toes.'

Berlioz had by now obviously had quite enough of 'The War March of the Priests' and presently led the way into the nave to the back pew where, it seemed, he kept a piece of old carpet which he occasionally chewed and threw about the church. Leaving him to his pastime, the organist pointed to a wall crammed with memorials of every period, shape, size and taste, and some with no taste at all. 'Most of these were our choir people,' he explained. 'This wall is sort of dedicated to the choir. We had a big choir years ago.'

'They had a job with the choir vestry then, didn't they?' I couldn't help observing.

He wagged a finger. 'Ah, the choir didn't have a vestry then – they used the belfry but it must have been awkward with the draught and the pigeons. That's why, about 100 years ago, someone paid to have our vestry built. He was our local butcher and was a great admirer of the choir. But then another admirer bought us the organ to replace the harmonium and that was so big that it took up most of the choir vestry to get it in.'

'That's unfortunate,' I said.

'Well' – the organist spread his hands philosophically – 'according to my grandfather, the organ was given by a man who was a vegetarian campaigner and he and the butcher never got on together.'

'Perhaps, one of these days, you may get another benefactor who will build a bigger vestry,' I said.

'Oh, we have,' he said. 'Unfortunately, we have. There's a man who moved into the manor house here a year or so ago and he's very keen on the church and keeps photographing it and writing about it, and he's offered to build us a new choir vestry with a piano, and room for rehearsals and space for a music library. I ask you!' He repeated the words aghast. 'A piano, rehearsals and a music library – whatever does he think we want all that for?'

'Might be useful!' I offered.

He shook his head and smiled forbearingly. 'We like our vestry how it is. It's our place,' he said. 'We don't want people butting in and littering it with pianos and things.'

The church door swung open suddenly and violently, and a large formidable-looking lady in tweeds and a cloak and pork-pie hat tramped in. She acknowledged the organist with the slightest jerk of the pork pie and took no notice of me apart from pushing me out of the way. The organist looked after her as she thrashed on up the aisle.

'Now, she's really going to help us over the vestry business,' he said. 'She can't stand the choir – says we're a completely unnecessary evil.'

'And that's going to help?' I queried.

'Not half,' he enthused. 'She's trying like mad to get this man to forget the vestry and build us a crèche for the kids of the people who come to the family service. She says children matter a lot more than types like us.'

'Ah!' I said.

He looked happy. 'She's a very persuasive lady. She'll get her way all right. She always does. I reckon no one will ever muck about with our choir vestry while she's around.'

13

The Infiltration

The new vicar at my friend James's village church is one of those whose fame or unpopularity go well ahead of them and who have, therefore, been thoroughly investigated by the whole congregation weeks before they arrive in the parish. Accordingly, on his induction as vicar, such a man can expect the parish attitudes towards him and his ideas to be solidly formulated and hardened, and all opinions firmly entrenched well ahead of his first sermon and letter in the parish magazine. The sermon and the letter, in any case, are traditionally dismissed as mere propaganda to lull the suspicions of all the unacceptable things the new incumbent really intends doing once fully in charge.

So the parish had been ready for the new vicar.

The altar servers were well prepared to defend their notions on correct ritual to the last genuflection; the men's society were more than ready for any confrontation regarding merging their group with the ladies' group; the flower-arranging ladies were not going to listen at all to the rumoured ideas about members' being obliged to attend a professional flower-arranging course before being let loose in the church with camouflaged plastic buckets and bunches of miscellaneous green stuff purloined from the overgrown vicarage garden. Also flatly rejected in advance was the new vicar's alleged habit of charging the church wardens to be 'really chummy' with newcomers, making them feel immediately 'one of the family' by ensuring that they signed a form giving all their details and professing interest in the free-will offering scheme. And long-established members of the congregation who wouldn't come to the modern jolly family service, but persisted in attending choral Matins only, and who refused to join any vital, forward-thinking parish groups, were on full alert to oppose any pressure to change their ways. Only the choir and organist and the bell-ringers were, predictably, not at all concerned about the advent of the new vicar, but then they'd always done just what they liked anyway and never took any notice of anyone. Not that the choir and bell-ringers have ever been in any kind of harmony. As part of the rich tapestry of church life they have been at loggerheads for years. The trouble is that the bell-ringers insist on ringing a full peal right up to the moment the service begins, while the organist, equally insistent, considers it his duty to 'create the proper devotional atmosphere' for the service by playing what he calls 'appropriate music' ten minutes before the service begins. What with the organist's idea of appropriate devotional music being firmly based on Strauss waltzes and military marches and the bell-ringers' policy being one of letting raw learner ringers 'have a go' in the team as soon as they can grab a rope without hanging themselves, the resultant villainous overture to the service has to be heard to be believed. Even the new vicar, a clever, calculating young cleric brimming with secret plans to change everything in the church that he can lay his hands on, but treading very softly during the first months of his ministry, has been known to question mildly whether such an evil uproar is really conducive to a devotional atmosphere, but James says that no one in the congregation has ever complained because none of them ever does anything devotional before the service anyway. When they arrive in church they all stand around in groups chatting about forthcoming parish get-togethers while their children run all over the place, and they only dive for their seats at the last moment when the choir shuffles in to start the service.

And smoothly weaving the rich tapestry into some sort of cohesive whole is the wonderful vicar's warden. Now there is a man! Vicar's wardens come in a variety of types and guises. There are those who relish the idea of holding an official position in the local church and making rules and ordering people about, and knowing what others don't know about the vicar's deep-laid plans for discontinuing Sunday Evensong, or ripping out all the pews and making the chancel into a concert platform. Others have not the faintest interest in the vicar's tradition-wrecking plans, or in the vicar himself. They just think it pleasant to have a special pew with a padded seat and their name on a brass-framed card. Then there are those, too public-spirited and accommodating for their own good, who find themselves pushed into the job by enthusiastic colleagues on the church council who are anxious to make quite sure that they don't get lumbered with it.

But the vicar's warden in James's church doesn't fall into any of these categories. When it comes to managing the parish (in the vicar's name of course), he's a near genius. He's single, large, middle-aged and comfortable-looking, always appears relaxed and pleasant, has a smile like the sunrise, has an ever-bubbling sense of humour and is indeed the ideal for anyone's favourite uncle. People like to talk to him. When he is consulted by the organist, the bell-ringers and other parish trouble-makers, the smile breaks forth and he either grips your hand in a knuckle-crushing grasp or hugs you bear-like, depending on whether you are male or female, old or young, and assures you, 'I am with you – I am right behind you – You've hit the nail on the head – Yes indeed!' Then he rolls off into the distance, smiling encouragingly, and you don't hear any more about your concerns or his support of them. But you still feel good about things and know that you are in the right because he is behind you and understands and appreciates.

Recently, after a particularly rowdy Sunday Matins (the choir traditionally favour the sort of Victorian hymns and anthems based on the more sensational and blood-thirsty passages of the Old Testament), during which the bell-ringers had carried on a chaotic peal well into the first hymn, the organist was much surprised to come upon the vicar's warden loitering in the choir vestry instead of beaming and (to use James's word) conning everyone in sight at the back of the church. The vicar's warden explained. Simply, he had decided that he wanted to join the choir. In tones of ringing sincerity and enthusiasm he explained to the organist that he had for years admired the choir from afar and only now had he found the courage to put himself forward as a possible member (back row of the chorus, of course!) of that very distinguished company. Truth to tell, this was the new vicar's first cautious move to impose his secret plans on the choir and in the course of the common good he had been acting deviously. In the strictest confidence he had suggested to his warden that working from within the choir he could, with his wonderful, loving, caring personality, eventually persuade the members of the choir to change their ways and ditch the awful music they bawled out every Sunday and embrace the lovely new 'praise songs' that he felt were essential for twenty-first-century Christian gatherings.

Caught completely off guard, the organist agreed that the warden could 'have a go' in the choir if he liked, and the warden, pressing home his advantage, suggested eagerly that perhaps he could try on a spare cassock there and then (no time like the present, what!). The organist, anxious to catch up with the rest of the choirmen already on their way to their post-Matins gathering at the Dog and Duck, hurriedly passed the new recruit over to a blatantly attractive choirgirl, who was endeavouring to extract a wad of dog-eared anthems for Evensong from the unbelievable chaos in the music cupboard. The choirgirl raised violet eyes to heaven, ceased her efforts with the dog-eared anthems, and turning a smile on the vicar's warden that unfailingly reduced all the younger male members of the choir to simpering supplicants, proceeded to fit him out with their one spare cassock, a long pensioned-off, faded, disintegrating wreck of a garment that was, however, still comparatively free from candle-grease and still retained two whole sleeves and one or two buttons. She stepped back to survey his tattered scarecrow figure with beaming enthusiasm. 'There!' she pronounced. 'You know, you look splendid, really splendid, a perfect fit – it's you! Oh yes, most attractive, you certainly must join the choir. You look absolutely right!' And her violet eyes were guileless. Vaguely the vicar's warden sensed that he'd at last met his match.

It is strange how things work out. James tells me that the vicar's warden has suddenly realized that he has a rather fine bass voice eminently suited to the choir's war-like Victorian anthems. Already he has sung some smaller solos and he's even taken part in a duet with the charmer with the violet eyes. He's not standing as vicar's warden next year so that he can give all his time to the choir. He is, of course, still as supportive as ever of the vicar, agreeing wholeheartedly with all his plots and aspirations. It has to be said though, that no great changes, or any change at all, are discernible in the music – or anywhere else in the parish for that matter.

But the new vicar is nothing if not optimistic. Everyone is becoming so friendly, even one or two of the bell-ringers now nod to him vaguely when they bump into him in the street. Everything will eventually work out well, he is sure. It really is a happy parish.

14

The Oasis and the Wilderness

Following my usual practice of endeavouring to sing in the local church choir whenever I am on holiday, I called one evening some years ago on the rector of a small Wiltshire village.

The rectory was a delightful Regency building, almost hidden behind walls that would have done justice to a prison.

Once inside the gates, the front garden was a joy to behold. There was nothing formal about it. It was really a back-to-nature effort, and consisted mainly of vast numbers of uninhibited hollyhocks interspersed with hordes of unchecked dandelions that were much bigger and more flamboyant than any I had ever dug out of the lawn at home.

The lawn in this case was unique and full of character, wandering all over the paths and halfway up the front steps. And gracing the whole scene, adding that indefinable old-world touch, there stood in the centre of the lawn a 20-ton traction engine.

The rector, opening the door and noting the admiration on my face, explained eagerly that he was the chairman of the local traction engine society which held those breathtaking, exciting races over ploughed fields every bank holiday.

I said I was grateful that at least *some* people were saving the steam-engine from extinction, and, beaming, he led me into a large kitchen-like apartment with a stone-flagged floor. As it was a rather chilly evening, he drew up a settle in front of a magnificent black and brass range which stretched along one entire wall.

The rector, a middle-aged unobtrusive type, was apparently a bachelor, and pointed out that notwithstanding its beauties, the house was perhaps just a little inconvenient for him, having 12 bedrooms, no bathrooms, no domestic staff, and the aforementioned range which burned about half a ton of coal a day and provided stone-cold water in every part of the house at all times.

No one lived with him, but in the cathedral-like stables at the rear of the rectory he nurtured a gigantic shire horse, which kept winning prizes at agricultural shows – and never did any work at all. It did, however, obviate the necessity of mowing the lawn.

The rector, who admitted that he was completely fascinated by Shire horses and traction engines, started to expand on the subjects, and as I also admire those symbols of massive power we would have gone on till midnight had I not suddenly recalled the purpose of my visit.

As I mentioned the choir, the rector's whole being seemed to change, and he became as a broken man. Shuddering as he forced a haggard smile, he stammered: 'Yes, we have a very good choir here – very enthusiastic – perhaps just a *little* – er – *overwhelming* at times.'

'Overwhelming?' I queried, and he explained.

The choir was really a kind of union, he said, and its members formed large majorities on the parochial church council and all the other committees in the parish. Consequently the choir ran the whole church. 'But a good bunch,' he ended dutifully. 'A good bunch.'

I was now very eager to meet this bunch, so the rector took me along to Evensong and left me in the choir vestry till some members should arrive. Two gentlemen soon appeared, and as they saw me, one politely inquired of the other in a fascinating brogue: 'What's 'e want?'

I was indeed impressed by the open-hearted welcome. After staring at me as if I were something from outer space, they shook hands with paralysingly friendly grasps. Even when they learned that I was an alto, they intimated very clearly that they didn't hold that against me: after all, I couldn't help it. I felt really at home.

Just before 6.30, when Evensong was due to commence, a little man who bore a striking resemblance to Napoleon Bonaparte suddenly called a meeting of the choir in a dark corner of the vestry.

Apparently someone had suggested removing the gravestones in the churchyard, and he wanted to know what everybody thought about this so that they could all think the same and solidly oppose the idea at the forthcoming church council meeting.

They all thought the same very quickly, and that problem being disposed of, there appeared to be just one other question to settle. This entailed gathering round a hymn book with much head-shaking. Then Napoleon went over to the rector and told him that the choir could not do as he had mildly suggested and sing the first hymn to the second tune because they had *always* sung the first hymn to the *first* tune.

The rector said he quite understood, and we all processed into the chancel.

The church was lighted by oil lamps on ornate brass standards. They shed a gentle, soothing light, and the heat was terrific.

To give them their due, the choir were first rate, and there was no doubt that the organist was a great improvement on his predecessor, a lady who had played the same two chants for the *Magnificat* and the *Nunc Dimittis* for 35 years. I began to enjoy myself immensely.

It was when we reached the anthem that we ran into the only little squall in the whole service. Goss's 'The Wilderness' was to be sung, and the bass soloist was Napoleon. Just as the rector made the announcement, Napoleon's lamp went out, and a kindly disposed man next to me quickly passed down his own lamp to take its place.

It was the worst thing he could have done. Evidently Napoleon interpreted the action as a suggestion that he couldn't sing the famous recitative without consulting the music, because halfway through the chorus I found the lamp thrust back into my hands, causing me to miss my place and nearly ruin the whole thing.

After the service the rector invited the choir to the rectory for a cup of tea. They thanked him and said they'd be along later. A meeting had been called to discuss Napoleon's faulty oil lamp.

15

It's an Ill Wind

I prefer the country to the seaside, but on one rare occasion I holidayed at a small but well-known south coast resort.

Owing to circumstances beyond the control of the motor-coach company – or anyone else for that matter – I arrived four and a half hours late in a state of suppressed fury. I was therefore in no mood to appreciate the bright little promenade, with its gaily painted lamp-standards between which were strung dozens of coloured electric light bulbs, and behind which there seemed to be almost as many beach photographers, who kept springing out on me and insisting on taking my photograph.

The place was thronging with people wearing funny paper hats which invited all and sundry to 'Kiss me quick' and 'Hold me tight', but as I merely wanted a good meal and a night's sleep I took no notice and hurried on.

After a brief pre-arranged call on the local vicar, during which I engineered an invitation to sing in the choir the next day, I retired to my guest-house.

I awoke much refreshed with a feeling that I was really going to enjoy this holiday. A terrific thunderstorm was in progress and the Sunday papers said that the weather would continue to deteriorate and that the further outlook was the same.

However, the rain had eased a little as church-time approached, and I again made my way along the bright little promenade. A large official noticeboard welcomed me to the sunshine and golden beaches of the town, and there followed a list of amenities designed to help me enjoy myself, but I couldn't quite make out what they were because the bottom of the board was veiled in a curtain of mud thrown up from the pavement by the force of the incessant rain.

Only one man sat on the beach, tastefully attired in bathing trunks and a trench coat with the collar turned up. But quite a large number of holiday-makers were wending their way to church. They were all trying to persuade themselves that they would have attended service even if the sun *had* been shining, and were looking very righteous as they parked their streaming umbrellas and hung their macs over the backs of pews.

I found the vicar in the vestry, but, although he had already made my acquaintance, he seemed at a loss to know who I was or what I wanted. Eventually, however, he obligingly introduced me to the organist as someone bearing a name quite unlike my own and coming from a place I'd never heard of. I, of course, righted the matter with the organist, who excused the vicar's lapse by explaining that I'd arrived at a very tricky time when he was engrossed in his usual Sunday-morning pastime of changing most of the hymns at the last minute and substituting different tunes for those that remained.

When the service was about to start, the organist, who appeared to be a very cultured and well-spoken man, called the choir together to give his final instructions. He said: 'I hope to goodness you lot will at least *try* to keep the "Smart in F" *Te Deum* in tune this Sunday, because last week it sounded something awful!'

Would they also please remember that this week all the collections were going to the choir outing fund. If they had to depend on the regular congregation who *knew* them, they naturally couldn't expect a penny, but luckily the weather had forced along a great many visitors who might be induced to give generously if only the choir's efforts were not too excruciating. It was a case of fooling most of the people *some* of the time. He appealed to the boys, therefore, to make an all-out effort to look as though they were normal and had a vague idea of what they were supposed to be doing. And would the altos, who seemed to imagine they were barn-owls calling to their mates, please soft-pedal the hooting, and the basses remember that they were supposed to be singers and not steamrollers.

Finally – just because the service was to conclude with the singing of 'All hail the power' to the tune 'Diadem', it was no excuse for the choir to imagine they were at a revivalist meeting or on a roundabout, so would they kindly refrain from going wild. Of course, the congregation would get into the usual fantastic muddle wondering whether to sing the long 'Crown Him' with the trebles and tenors, or the short sharp 'Crown Him' with the altos and basses, but if any of the boys were caught openly laughing at them they'd cop it good and proper afterwards.

Noting the look of admiration on my face, a fellow alto beamed at me joyously. 'Terrific, isn't he?' he enthused, 'we wouldn't miss his little Sunday morning homilies for the world. He didn't mention the tenors this week but last week he called them the biggest lot of . . .' But I never heard what the tenors were. The vicar weighed in just then, and shepherded us all into the chancel.

The church was packed. I am sure everyone enjoyed the service, particularly 'All hail the power'. As the organist had forecast, the congregation did get mixed up with the 'Crown Hims' which came at us on all sides like pistol-shots, but such was the impact of the flamboyant Victorian tune that everyone felt impelled to sing to the last note – flat or sharp, in time or out.

The composer of 'Diadem', James Ellor, was an obscure hat-maker and railway labourer who wrote only one tune in his life. He thought it would go no further than the tiny country chapel where he led the choir, but it went round the world and it worked a miracle – it made Church of England congregations forget themselves, forget their weather, and sing!

No Plot – Just an Observation

My friend Harry says, for him, the very attractive thing about his village church choir is that, in a fast-changing very unstable world, the choir are fervently traditional in all things. They've been like that since the middle of the nineteenth century when the choir was founded as a male voice ensemble by an ex-choirboy, the landlord of the Goat and Compasses, and they have become ever more traditional over the years. Admittedly, some lady singers have found their way into the male stronghold in recent times and the splendid decorative oil lamps in the choir stalls have long been electrified, but happily the ladies have carried on driving the organist mad with their vocal efforts just as thoroughly as the men do, and the electrified lamps still *look* like oil lamps, so there are no difficulties about keeping tradition alive.

Of course, there's always the vicar for the choir to deal with. The bachelor priest in Harry's parish these days is a youngish, quietly enthusiastic man of the modern school who doesn't appear to appreciate the choir's fervent traditional stand, which, indeed, he secretly regards as a product of a stick-in-the-mud mentality ('Such a pity, because I'm sure that at heart, deep down, there are some very nice people in our choir'), which is seriously impeding the progress of his programme of vital new forms of church services that he plans to introduce as soon as possible. Nevertheless, the vicar is a kind, respected man whose whole being, according to the young impressionable lady secretary to the parochial church council, 'radiates peace and loving togetherness' (and the vicar is quite good looking too). Harry reckons that, being so radiant, the vicar really does try his hardest to appreciate the choir's loyal presence and input at every service that he is in the process of transforming into a near non-musical discussion group wrestling with urgent questions like 'What is wrong with the Church and how can we put it right, apart from giving more and more money each month?'

But for one particular traditional service the vicar really gives his whole-hearted support – the choir's annual choral evensong in honour of Arnold the organist's umpteenth birthday. Indeed, on this occasion the vicar actually preaches from the pulpit instead of wandering among the congregation on their orange plastic chairs, which have replaced the pews, and addressing various members personally. ('Now, what do *you* make of the Archbishop's words, Fred?') This is also the one occasion in the year when the vicar lets the choir sing their favourite warlike Victorian hymns all about charging for the God of battle, and mighty armies crushing the sinful and causing Satan's hosts to flee, and the organist is free to play 'The Ride of the Valkyrie' as the voluntary at the end of the service. The organ is a very powerful one and at his birthday celebrations Arnold rides the Valkyrie at full blast, completely obliterating the gentle messages of peace and joy that the vicar is wafting to the departing, hand-shaking congregation, obliterating also the annual complaint of the usual half-dozen hand-shakers whose expressions of agony and fury, directed at the raging Wagnerian organist, are totally misread by the vicar, who always smiles bravely and mouths, 'Yes, splendid, wonderful, isn't he!'

I'd not visited Harry's village previously and being now invited to join the choir for the organist's latest birthday celebrations, I arrived in good time at the church. It was a nicely proportioned little early-Victorian building, sitting tidily and with a sort of self-satisfied air in a well-kept churchyard where all the gravestones were intact and upright and a large tabby cat posed regally, sunning himself on the top step of the war memorial. As I paused, enjoying my lovely, peaceful surroundings, the church vestry door opened and a tall schoolmasterly-looking man strode up to me. He seemed to know who I was, introducing himself as the vicar's warden and said that Harry was sorting out a cassock and surplice for me so that I could sit with the choir during the service. He was the sort of person, you felt, that everyone *had* to take notice of, a man of impressive presence – although I noticed the tabby completely ignored that presence and continued looking regal, wholly unaffected.

'Our choir are *very* important to the parish,' asserted the warden firmly. 'We can learn so *much* from them. They are *vital* to the future life of our parish as we move positively further into the exciting adventurous twenty-first century.' He fixed me with a fiery eye. 'Y'see, our choir are a *blatant*, ever present example of human stagnation – a stark warning to us of what happens when people exist absolutely stultified in the inborn belief that what has been done for years shall go on being done and everything is as it's supposed to be. Our choir are a challenge to our forward-looking parish and vicar to be ever vigilant, alive, not to be left behind in the thrilling development of the all-embracing life of the church – the challenging, difficult ever-changing situations . . .'

Harry arrived with my cassock and surplice and the vicar's warden bowed himself away and hurried to help an elderly choirman as he tugged a veteran motor-scooter into the vestry. Harry has a sparkling smile. 'So you met our vicar's warden! Has he had a word about the moribund members of the choir?' I explained to him how important the choir were to the whole parish in demonstrating the evils of being choir persons who boorishly wouldn't go along with the vicar's way of forging ahead and changing everything. Harry laughed. 'Oh, the vicar's warden, he's a lovely bloke really. We all like him. Just gets a bit upset when the vicar wants to cut out a hymn to do some more talking and our organist won't let him.'

We entered the choir vestry. Harry helped me on with my cassock and surplice and introduced me to four or five choir members of varying ages, including the inevitable respected veteran singer present in every choir who's been there for an eternity and always sings flat and insists that things were better in *his* day when the choir kept the services going at a cracking, brisk no-nonsense pace and weren't slowed down halfway through by everyone in the congregation shaking hands and chatting all over the place.

Harry went off to put out the service music in the choir stalls and I suddenly found myself cut off at the back of the vestry by the local respected veteran. 'You'd some-times not know that the choir are here at all,' he began immediately. 'The vicar is so taken up with what he's going to say about exciting new-type Sunday forums which he plans to substitute in place of morning service that he doesn't realize we are here till we all get in his way processing into church.'

'What a carry on!' I said.

'Oh, but he's always very nice and apologetic,' the veteran assured me. 'Last time, after he had failed to spot us in the vestry, he reminded the congregation how privileged they were in having us around to sing their praises for them, and he took us all for a drink after the service ...'

A few moments before the special service for the organist was due to begin, the vicar reluctantly stopped blocking the church porch by waylaying and chatting up members of the arriving congregation and whisked up the aisle to the choir vestry. 'Good, jolly good to see you all,' he beamed at us. 'I know our choir will always be here, ever ready and keen to sing to us through the service. Wonderful indeed, yes!'

'He's rather overwhelming when he meets us on Sunday mornings,' Harry observed. 'What he most likely means is, "I suppose we've got to put up with you lot bawling archaic psalms and outmoded Victorian hymns and reading your Sunday papers during my sermon when the precious time should all be used in vital discussion of *things that really matter*" – y'see the vicar doesn't like singing – he can't sing in any case, but he *does* like talking.'

Well, the choir did put on a really enthusiastic and enjoyable show for the organist's birthday celebration (enjoyable for the choir anyway), and the vicar went over the top with his most extravagant words of praise for the organist 'whose brilliant, inspiring tuition maintains the splendid choir you see before you today'.

And then, back in the choir vestry after the service, I was suddenly struck by the thought that, on this, his special day, we hadn't yet laid eyes on Arnold. I questioned Harry. He smiled. 'Ah! Should have told you. Likes to be a bit exclusive, does our Arnold. He comes in at the back of the chancel and goes up the iron staircase to the organ loft. Sometimes we don't see him at all on Sundays and the vicar can't get hold of him to change a hymn at the last minute. Did you notice the organ loft, high up and dark between those two fearful-looking gargoyles, with only a small light over the manuals? All we see of Arnold is a monstrous spooky shadow (Harry is a devotee of horror films) but we can *feel* his presence with his gimlet eyes boring into us and boring more and more furiously as the service continues and we carry on making all the mistakes that he warned us not to make at Friday night's choir practice. After his voluntary at the end of a service he gets down his iron stairway like lightning and starts shouting at any choir member who has failed to escape in time.' Harry shook his head and chuckled. 'He's a nice man though – quite odd, but nice, and he's got a nice wife to keep him in order. She's a lovely roly-poly lady with rosy cheeks and laughing eyes, and when Arnold starts shouting at people she just says, "Arnold, shut up!" and he does. Then she says, "Tell them at choir practice that they were very good on Sunday – inspiring. They won't believe you but it makes a nice atmosphere in the choir."' 'And does Arnold do that?' I asked. 'Arnold does that,' he said.

All too soon, Harry was walking me back to the station on my way home. 'So,' I said, 'who's going to win the new-style services contest – the pushy vicar or the stick-in-the-mud choir?' '*Please*,' reprimanded Harry, '– the forward-thinking vicar and the traditional choir – well – neither really. The congregation will win. Most of them come to church on a Sunday because that's what they do and happily partake in whatever is offered, including several cups of tea and gossip at the end of the service. Some of them wouldn't mind doing a bit more talking instead of listening to the vicar's sermon and others couldn't imagine singing half a dozen hymns without the choir to sing them for them if you see what I mean.' I said I grasped what he meant. 'So,' reasoned Harry, 'as long as the present situation carries on in its civilized, democratic manner, everyone will be happy, and we shall end up with the choir still singing all the archaic psalms and outmoded hymns and the vicar bouncing about among the orange plastic chairs posing personal questions.'

As we were passing the lychgate, the vicar came through beaming his most eager smile. 'It was so *good* to have you with us in the choir this morning,' he enthused. We shook hands and I assured him that I would be back there in their choir again and again. 'I so enjoy the vigorous singing,' I said. And the vicar bravely retained his eager smile.

17

Smell the Difference

The receptionist at the hotel where I was staying said that the old parish church had been destroyed by bombing in the Second World War, but they now had a replacement which after all these years they still called 'the nice new one'. She'd never been inside it. 'No time these days, somehow' – but everyone told her it was very nice. She was sure I would find it very nice.

So I set out to look for the very nice new church and very nearly made a fool of myself. It was only at the bottom of the road, but after half an hour of futile wandering I was on the point of returning to the receptionist to report that I couldn't find it, when I spotted the noticeboard. I had passed the church about half a dozen times, but had thought it was a biscuit factory, or something to do with the council's waste disposal unit.

There it stood, a large concrete and glass cube, attached at one corner to a smaller concrete and glass cube, and surrounded by a yellow gravel path. And the noticeboard was no less unique. It was in the shape of a triangle, supported on a steel tube and coloured red and white. Notices covered its entire surface. There were large posters announcing bingo sessions, discos and a public meeting about council tax, and at the narrowest angle of the triangle, tucked away behind a bush, was a shy little reminder that services were held in the church.

I entered the place through the plate-glass double doors, and was gaping about me in amazement when I noticed, almost in my pocket, a short, middle-aged woman with blue hair and a jutting chin. She glared at me and demanded: 'Well, what do you think of our church?' What did I think of this adventurous break with tradition, this lightness and airiness? Wasn't I thrilled – absolutely thrilled? She obviously didn't expect an answer, because, without taking a breath, she told me that of course I was. I realized, she said, that the church today had no time for backward looking and thinking. It must forge ahead with modern buildings, modern methods, modern *thought* . . .

We then forged ahead up the main aisle, and my self-appointed guide proudly pointed out the glories of the square concrete pillars and the delightfully unadorned roof girders. She insisted on walking behind me and instructing me from under my arm. She wore flat, unpolished shoes which were so long that they kept scraping my heels as she drove me round the building from eyesore to eyesore.

We halted before one of the floor-to-ceiling windows. 'No dim religious light here,' she gloated. 'All pure, honest daylight through clean clear glass.' And certainly the windows admitted the maximum amount of light. They were also very useful if you got fed up with the sermon, because they enabled you to amuse yourself unobtrusively by watching the would-be passengers fuming in the bus queue or car drivers cursing at the traffic lights.

The woman was now throwing back her blue head and breathing ecstatically. I thought for a panic-stricken moment that she was going to faint or throw a fit, but I needn't have worried. She hadn't finished with me yet. Her voice softened, and she smiled almost kindly at me as she asked mysteriously, 'And don't you notice something else different about this church?'

I was in rather a quandary here, because I felt sure that if I did mention some of the things I'd noticed different about the place she'd be quite capable of ejecting me forcibly. So I just stood there, smiling and stammering. 'Well – of course . . .'

Luckily she couldn't stop talking for long, and came to my rescue eagerly. 'No churchy smell!' she enthused. 'No fustiness! Good clean air!' She was quite right of course. Judging by the good clean smell I should imagine that the person who had recently mopped the floor had upset a whole bottle of carbolic in the water.

And now, just for a moment as we stood there sniffing, I had my first chance to lead the conversation.

'Where does the choir sit?' I asked.

She was still enraptured with the carbolic, and I had caught her off her guard. She became quite annoyed.

'We've put them out of the way in the gallery,' she said shortly. 'The Victorians paraded them in the chancel. We've nothing Victorian here.' Then smartly she took control again. 'This way,' she commanded, prodding me into the vestry.

I had the sudden vivid impression that I was entering a large shoebox. At one end a bearded young man was sorting through some music manuscripts. My guide introduced him to me as the organist, and he came forward vaguely and shook hands. Looking through me, he said that he liked to feel that his was the finest choir in the diocese. He waved his arms round the walls, which were peppered with prize certificates, and said I could see for myself. He then treated me to a lecture on church music and explained that all the neighbouring choirs and organists were morons, who degraded themselves by pandering to the unspeakably sentimental taste of their congregations.

When he eventually dismissed me, the woman saw me off down the yellow gravel path. She was telling me that in the morning I should be awakened by the sound of bells, but it would not be produced by the wasteful employ of eight ringers. Here again the church was up-to-date: they used a stereo recording.

On Sunday morning I sang in the choir of a nearby church. It was a solid red brick Victorian effort, filled with painted texts and loaded with plaques. The dim religious light filtered through stained-glass windows depicting saintly gentlemen wearing red and blue nightgowns and dinner-plate halos – memorials to a century of Indian Army colonels and local tradesmen.

An outsized brass lectern-eagle presided magnificently at the chancel steps, and, yes, there was just the faint suggestion of a church smell. The choir sang a popular and thoroughly hackneyed setting of the *Te Deum*. Even the congregation knew it. I felt at home.

18

From East to West, from Shore to Shore

I was quite sure I knew where St Mark's was. I wasn't really familiar with that particular suburb of London, but I'd passed through it hurriedly a number of times (it was one of those places that you *do* pass through hurriedly if you possibly can), and always I'd been quite certain that the large red-brick edifice that reared up on the rising ground behind the brewery and looked so uncannily like a blast furnace was indeed St Mark's.

A journalist friend of mine was preparing a series of articles for our parish magazine on neighbouring churches and I'd volunteered to take a photo of St Mark's for him to illustrate his latest contribution. I'd arrived in the town early on Saturday morning so that I could get a picture more or less unimpeded by the regular solid mass of traffic which, a little later, would encircle the church in blue diesel fumes and cursing drivers, and block every road for miles.

I was already adjusting my camera outside the church and trying to decide on which angle would most likely tone down the unique blast furnace effect, when I spotted the noticeboard. It announced that gentlemen with unobjectionable voices were needed in the choir, there was to be a jumble sale on a date that had already passed two months ago, and that a film strip on some place that the rain had washed off the home-made poster would be shown in place of the sermon next Sunday. But the notice-board was not headed 'St Mark's'. It said, quite clearly, 'St John's'.

I must have been looking particularly lost, because an extraordinarily cheerful bus-inspector suddenly appeared and asked in a kindly voice if he could help me. I asked him where St Mark's was, and in an even kindlier voice he said he didn't know. He suggested, however, that I should try more towards the centre of the town. There was, he explained, next door to his bus garage, a religious kind of building with pointed windows and gravestones and things, and *that* might be St Mark's.

I thanked him very much, and after negotiating three or four of those suicidal pedestrian crossings of which the traffic takes no notice whatsoever – not even when the lights brightly invite you to 'Cross now' – and climbing in and out of some nice, new safe pedestrian subways, which kept on bringing me out on the wrong side of the road or into the middle of a furious bus queue, I eventually chanced upon the inspector's religious kind of build-ing. This turned out to be a splendid eighteenth-century church, surrounded by some most interesting tombs, and a noticeboard entirely covered with a yellow and purple poster which asked me in letters a foot high where I thought I was going. The place was securely locked, and was called St Peter's.

By this time I was feeling a little down-hearted and, as is always the case when I feel a little down-hearted, I decided to find a cup of tea and, perhaps, something to eat. It was still quite early, and the only place open in the vicinity which remotely resembled a café was one of those establishments which always seem to belong to someone called Joe, and to be constantly filled with numerous large gentlemen who are supposed to be digging up the road for the Gas Board, or filling in a hole for the Water Board. I was drawn inside by the glorious aroma of newly cooked ham, but that particular ham must have been reserved for the regulars because, when I ordered a ham sandwich, the girl behind the counter said there wasn't any ham, and eventually presented me with a semi-transparent slice of corned beef imprisoned between two brutal great chunks of stale bread.

A young man who had been grimly concentrating on a journal devoted to greyhounds, and stirring his tea with a screwdriver, looked round a case of bloated cream doughnuts and asked the girl if she was going to be at the Devil's Cavern Beat Club that evening, and she said she was, but not with him. She said she wouldn't be seen dead with him on the same bus, never mind at the Devil's Cavern. She picked up a large, brown enamel teapot, and started slopping tea all over some cups and saucers which didn't match, as she gazed trancelike at a full-page magazine picture of the current pop-singing idol, a young man who appeared to consist entirely of an extravagant amount of long hair and outsize black glasses.

After a few ecstatic moments, the girl put down the teapot, mopped up the tea, and smiled lovingly at a damp patch on the wall above my head.

'I wonder,' I said brightly, 'if you could tell me where I could find St Mark's church.' She jerked her head down and stared at me, horrified.

'Wot!' she asked incredulously.

'St Mark's,' I repeated encouragingly.

'Just a minute,' she managed to mumble, and disappeared through a bead-curtained doorway, where she shortly reappeared with a large, round unshaven character who could have been none other than Joe himself. They stood there, festooned with beads, their faces full of suspicion. Suddenly Joe seemed to make up his mind. He humoured me gently.

'Looking for a church, are yer?' he asked, not unkindly. 'It's not Sunday yet, y'know!' His jolly face looked almost cherubic. 'There's that church at the top of the hill. Used to go there to Sunday school, donkey's years ago. That might be St Mark's – it's either St Mark's or the Salvation Army. We used to sing like mad every Sunday afternoon. We enjoyed it. No telly in them days, y'see.'

It was the Salvation Army. I came back down the hill by a different route from the one by which I had ascended. There was still a chance of spotting St Mark's, I considered, so long as I kept my eyes open, and didn't ask anyone who thought they knew where it was. But all I spotted was a man wearing a homburg hat with a big hole in the brim, who was piling an old iron bedstead on to his cart and complaining bitterly to his horse. 'Wanted ten bob for this lot! Ten bob! Lucky to get it taken away at all. Ten bob! Blimey!' I couldn't resist the temptation. I gave him a helping hand with the bed, and asked him if he could direct me to St Mark's.

'Ten bob!' he repeated indignantly. 'I think it's gone. I think it got bombed in the war. They've built some council flats and the supermarket there now. Ten blinkin' bob! Where did you say – St Faith's?'

I wandered on. I took my journalist friend's crumpled note from my wallet. There it was, as clear as the nose on your face – 'If you could get a good photo of the church, I should be most grateful. Anyone will tell you where it is – St Matthew's.' St Matthew's! I gazed, crushed, at the note. I must be getting senile even quicker than I imagined. Too old at 40, they said. Now my memory was going.

A policeman was regarding me sternly. He was very young and very smart. He didn't smile helpfully when I asked him the way to St Matthew's.

'I'm very new here,' he pronounced in a very official voice. 'The only church I know is the one across the road.' He pointed to a portly Victorian pile which had seemed suddenly to appear between the King's Head and the Odeon. 'But *that's* St Mark's.'

19

Wedding Break

I was enjoying myself hugely at one of those country church fêtes where everybody is expected to throw little wooden balls into non-receptive buckets and guess how many beans there are in a jam jar.

You are generally inveigled into performing these antics by a most charming maiden whose smile reduces the men, at least, into simpering idiots. Under the sweet influence they become more and more reckless in their efforts to please, and with their money, the organ fund or the beetle-in-the-tower fund prospers exceedingly.

Naturally the hard core of the fête consists of the colourful stalls where you can purchase a wide variety of things you don't want, which you can then hand back for the next jumble sale.

To add to the romantic excitement of the whole thing, there is often a fortune-teller at your service. She rejoices in a name like Madame Hamboni, and claims descent from a long line of fortune-tellers who foretold the fates of all the crowned heads of Europe. Actually she is a local lady who, of course, knows the business of everyone in the village from constant consultation at the local post office. Heavily disguised with cocoa and earrings she pretends she is learning about you for the first time as she gazes into the depths of her upturned goldfish bowl.

The lady at this fête was doing a brisk trade dispensing promises of dark lovers, unlimited travel and tons of money, and I was about to join the queue for my share when my friend with whom I was holidaying suddenly appeared and grabbed my arm.

'Come on,' he gasped, 'Here's a chance to do your stuff. Our choir has got a job.' He was in a tremendous hurry, and I had the greatest difficulty in discovering what was going on as he dragged me all over the fête-ground, rounding up members of the church choir.

As far as I gathered, it appeared that a dreadful mistake had been made at a neighbouring church. Owing to a confusion of dates, the choir and organist had gone off to a music festival at which they always won first prize, and a fashionable wedding due to take place within the hour was in danger of being left high and dry.

As a last resort their vicar had appealed for help to our choir. He knew that they never went to music festivals. They never went anywhere beyond their own church where they were well liked and understood by the congregation. For no matter how flat the congregation sang – and they had to be heard to be believed – they never sang quite as flat as the choir, and were therefore always filled with a false and pleasant pride in their vocal chords.

My friend said something about 'transport laid on', and shepherded about 20 uncomprehending choristers towards a disreputable horse-box. This was the conveyance of an outsized Suffolk Punch horse named Theodore the Tank, who had won the cart-horse derby held at the fête earlier in the afternoon. We clambered in behind him, and within a few moments were lurching on our way.

We made a brief stop at our church to collect our psalters, which were differently pointed from those at the neighbouring church. In no time at all an obliging little choirboy flung them into the back of the horse-box in the same reverent manner that they had been flung about the choir stalls for the last half-century.

As I picked them up and brushed the straw from them, a man who had been leaning nonchalantly on the rear end of Theodore and eating a bag of crisps, asked mildly where we were going, and I told him I thought it was to a wedding. Falling heavily against me and dropping his crisps as Theodore decided to move, he said that it would be a nice change because he was getting fed up with the fête anyway.

Discreetly spreading petrol fumes and straw along the bridal path, our horse-box lumbered up to the church behind a Daimler full of delicious bridesmaids. We followed these up a red carpet at a respectable distance and were soon fitting ourselves out from the super choir's elegant collection of robes, much to the disgust of a lordly verger who had obviously taken a violent dislike to choristers who smelt of horses and never went to music festivals.

The wedding itself was quite unremarkable. There was the usual nervous bridegroom waiting for the usual confident (late) bride. And there were the two families set in opposing camps on each side of the main aisle. When the bride eventually arrived on the arm of her father, she looked what the press unfailingly describe as 'radiant', and this seemed to have an effect on the still bemused choir who now appeared to realize for the first time why they were present, and proceeded to lead her up the aisle at a smart shamble.

The picture was slightly varied at this point by one of our basses, who appeared plodding solemnly up and down the choir stalls giving out our ragged psalters, and by the organist who was playing something which sounded like the 'Post Horn Gallop'.

Whether the congregation realized we were not the famed, prize-winning choir that should have been singing, I don't know, but they looked quite pleased with our elephantine efforts, and at the close of the service some even thanked us.

By this time Theodore the Tank had been taken home, and his horse-box was waiting to return us to the fête.

As we left, the official photographer was losing his temper posing the wedding party like statues round the church door. People with cameras and unmanageable children kept getting in his way, and two old ladies were throwing confetti over everyone within reach.

20

Our Traditional Carol Concert

'The trouble with you,' said my friend, the village church organist and a musician of the modern school, 'is that you are a Philistine.'

He was lovingly thumbing through one of those Christmas carol books in which the editors have so arranged and reharmonized the well-known, old, simple carols that they are transformed into nightmares of ear-splitting discords for double choir, full organ and as many other instruments as you can find. Generally, the congregation who have to endure them don't seem to recognize the original tune, and all but the most advanced members of the choir haven't the faintest idea of which part to sing, or when. But few Philistines like being actually labelled Philistines, so they all make out that they understand and thoroughly approve of the whole idea.

'Now take this, for instance,' enthused my friend, turning to a very simple little children's carol which had been inflated into something between a Handel grand chorus and a test-piece for a brass band contest, 'I reckon that even you couldn't fail to be moved by this.'

I reckoned I could.

But in spite of my pronounced Philistine leanings, my friend never gives me up as quite hopeless. He said it was most fortunate that the vicar had developed flu just at this time and that I had been able to come along to take over the task of subduing his choir probationers at the annual carol concert that evening.

As usual, the probationers were to sit in the audience and try to learn something from the fully fledged members of the choir who were, of course, singing at the concert together with a number of other choirs from the surrounding districts. My friend said that this year the carols chosen were so medieval and so beautiful that he was sure that somewhere a responsive chord would be struck in even my dreadful Victorian soul.

A little before 7 o'clock that evening, I herded the probationers into the village hall, where a tall, thin, gushing lady with a sort of army haircut kindly enquired who we were and kindly explained that there had been some little muddle about the seating arrangements, and that our seats had all been allotted to the supporters of a rival choir, who flatly refused to move. She assured us, however, that she had managed to reserve some equally good seats for us, and ushered us into a corner at the back of the hall, where the light had gone out and some pensioned-off church chairs of the sagging straw-seat variety were grouped around a shamefaced-looking billiard table, on which were set a line of bursting hassocks.

'There,' she chirruped comfortingly, 'you can all make yourselves at home here very well, I'm sure.' She said that the very small probationers could sit up on the billiard table so that they could get a good view. A few minutes later the concert commenced in a really rousing manner with the singing of 'O come, all ye faithful' (audience allowed to join in the singing of this one) with the village church choir on the platform, accompanied by my friend at the piano, a lady on a violin and a big cheerful-looking, red-headed young man who appeared to be in the very early stages of learning to be a timpanist.

We in the audience managed to disregard the timpani and to get well ahead of the violin. We were, indeed, even a shade ahead of the piano until the last verse, when the choir started to rise above us into a specially written descant, which eventually rose so high that it threw us all off key, and left us floundering helplessly among the final 'O comes'.

Anyway, a reed-like, fair young curate came out onto the stage and said we'd done jolly well, and then announced that a ladies' choir from some nearby village (famous for its early Norman church and its parish council, who refused to have street lamps in the village street) would now sing a very beautiful carol – very beautiful indeed. I think he was about to say more but, as he spoke, a procession of middle-aged ladies wearing long, flowing white dresses had been trailing onto the stage, and now, grouped tightly together, they started singing and swaying backwards and forwards, eyes fixed on their conductor, who was also swaying backwards and forwards as she lashed at the air with something that looked like a brass paper-knife.

The carol consisted of a large number of 'tra-las' and humming sounds, with a line or two of Latin thrown in here and there, and went on for so long that I had forcibly to restrain two of the probationers in front of me who were about to start a fight, presumably to pass the time until the next choir came on.

When at last the paper-knife had beaten out the last tra-la, the young curate, who by now appeared to be going into ecstasies, leapt onto the stage and told us something about the words of which he referred to as 'that truly lovely little gem of a carol'. Apparently they were from a genuine late-sixteenth-century manuscript which someone had found under the waiting room of a genuine late-nineteenth-century railway station. The curate said that he himself had had the honour of composing the music, which had come to him in a most wonderful, serene way last Boxing Day while he was helping with the washing up after the youth club party.

The next singers to take the platform were the village Sunday school choir. It was supposed to be drawn from the Sunday school but, in fact, included the whole Sunday school. An ability to sing had nothing to do with membership of the Sunday school choir. If a pupil was left out, its parents were apt to write a strong letter to the superintendent about victimization, or to send the child to another school and refuse to give anything to the vicar's Easter Offering.

The choir clattered onto the stage and formed themselves into a half-circle under the iron eyes of the vicar's wife, a large grimly smiling lady who, while she didn't actually push them about violently, nevertheless had a very firm grasp of the situation.

The young curate, who was beginning to recover a little from his ecstasy over the late-sixteenth-century carol, announced that the Sunday school choir would now sing 'Once in royal David's city'. He didn't seem half as keen about this one, possibly because it could be found in any hymn book, and had certainly not been discovered under a floor. But he nevertheless gave a charming smile to a little girl with a doll-like face and wearing a huge scarlet bow in her hair, who stepped forward to sing the opening verse.

She assumed an angelic expression, clasped her hands primly in front of her, and piped up with the coolest confidence.

It was just then that I noticed I was being firmly pushed off my chair and realized that two ladies, late-comers to the audience, were planting themselves next to me. Having taken her seat and half of mine, the nearest one settled back comfortably, tore the cellophane from a pound-box of chocolates, and announced to her friend, obviously a stranger to the village, 'This is our village hall. We had a tin hut before this, and I used to get absolutely frozen at the winter whist drives.'

'Where a mother laid her baby,' sang the angelic child.

'What a pretty little girl – no, I don't want one if they're hard centres,' said the friend.

'She's a little devil, really,' replied my neighbour.

'She reminds me of your Emily when she was a kid,' said the friend.

'For he is our childhood's pattern,' bawled the full choir.

'That's the vicar's wife up there with 'em,' pointed out my neighbour, tearing some more wrappings from the chocolates and dropping them on my knees.

'Seems to be in charge all right,' said the friend.

My neighbour tried to examine the inside of a chocolate in the half-light. 'You should have had this one – it's a soft centre – coffee cream. I can't stand coffee cream – well, course, she's in charge of everything in this parish. Can't just be a member of anything. Must be the chairman.'

'I don't like the look of that boy at the back of the choir,' decided the friend, 'the one who keeps shoving the boys in front of him. Proper little gangster, he's going to be.'

'He's our police-sergeant's boy,' said my neighbour.

'All in white shall wait around,' announced the choir in a final roar. The carol concert continued in its time-honoured manner, the audience standing from time to time to join in the singing of the well-known carols and sitting dumbly through the others, wondering what on earth they were all about and how much longer they'd take.

On this occasion there were the exceptions as far as the dumbness was concerned. The fascinating conversation between the two ladies next to me carried on unabated through the entire programme and a whole pound of chocolates. At the end of the concert I knew all that really mattered about everyone in the parish, even though I'd long surrendered my half chair to an outsized handbag, a fur jacket and an empty chocolate box, and was standing at some distance against a wall. The voices carried so well.

'Of course,' said my friend, as we drove away from the village hall, 'our vicar is dead against choirs and organists. Says they're unnecessary. Do you know . . .'

'Yes,' I butted in. 'I do. He thinks the congregation should all sing together like they do at cup finals, and that his voice is so good that nothing else is needed to lead them. And if he had his way, he'd burn all organists at the stake on a bonfire made of copies of all the anthems and settings ever composed.'

My friend gaped at me in wonderment.

'Yes, but how do you know all that? You haven't been down here since we've had this vicar.'

'I also know about the recent disgraceful occasion when you fell asleep during the bishop's sermon,' I continued. 'They had to wake you up to play the next hymn – and you played the next but one, and flung the whole place into confusion. Things filter through, you know. Things filter through.'

21

Ignored No Longer!

I hadn't seen Olley for many months when I recently, quite by chance, came upon him at a London station, where he appeared to be trapped in an automatic ticket barrier that had malfunctioned. A member of the station staff was doing his best to release Olley while apologizing profusely for the offending apparatus which, he said, had caused a number of screamingly funny incidents since an expert had attended to it a few days ago. Olley was entering into the fun of the whole situation while desperately trying to reshape a huge bouquet of exotic flowers that had been seriously battered by the cruel limbs of the barrier. Then he saw me as I passed through a neighbouring barrier with no ill effect.

Olley and I are old choir friends who have kept in touch for over 40 years. Nowadays he is a big noise in the church choir of the village to which he and his wife retired some years ago after busy City careers. Olley regarded the wrecked bouquet sadly. 'I'm in town for my great-aunt's 90th birthday gathering,' he explained. 'What's she going to say to this, 'er . . .' 'Mangled mess?' I suggested. 'Yes, exactly,' he agreed. 'What's she going to say to *that*?'

We suddenly realized that we hadn't met for a long time and that this meeting was a pleasant surprise – apart from Olley's great-aunt's battered bouquet of course – and that we both had a little time to spare. Accordingly, we quickly ensconced ourselves in a nearby coffee bar with mugs of a sort of coffee with much cream and grated chocolate on top. From choirboy days we had always been much taken with mugs of a sort of coffee with much cream and grated chocolate on top . . .

I was first in asking the question one of us always asks when we meet after a lengthy period: 'And how's the choir going?'

Now, let it be known that Olley is a choirman – a thundering basso-profundo – of the old school. Well, his whole choir are of the old school and as firmly established as their flamboyant Victorian choir stalls from where they regularly perform rousingly – always rousingly, whatever the nature of the music, much to the misery of occasional new curates who yearn for church services of a quieter meditative nature with whispered medieval melody. It is true to say that the choir have a genuine affectionate attachment to the choir stalls, which provide a refuge where they can relax and read their Sunday papers quite unnoticed by the congregation, during the vicar's Sunday sermon.

Olley gingerly spooned cream and grated chocolate from the top of his mug. 'Actually we've got a bit of bother coming up,' he confided. 'The choir will have to stand up and be counted, like when the vicar tries to sneak in a new hymn tune at the last moment before Matins.' He dealt further with the cream and grated chocolate with obvious huge delight before returning to his subject. Apparently, a few months ago, a most unusual event took place. A newcomer to the village, an early retired police-man with a glorious tenor voice, had joined the choir, a soloist whom the organist had over the years only dared dream about in his most imaginative moments. The choir welcomed him unreservedly and vigorously. Anyone who could help them raise the roof Sunday by Sunday and drown out the vicar's terrible tones and the operatic shrieking of the veteran twin ladies in the front pew was very welcome. Olley told me, 'Our soprano solo girl is quite overawed by the new tenor. She says his enthusiasm and love of music shines forth from his eyes and lights his whole countenance with joy. She always goes all sort of dramatic when she talks about music. Rose, one of our alto ladies, says it's because she has a beautiful, musical soul.' Olley looked puzzled. 'I don't know about that – I think it's because our new tenor is nice looking and quite a bit younger than the rest of the choir men.'

'So, anyway,' I led, 'on the whole, the choir are flourishing, and that must be good.' 'Ah!' Olley raised a warning hand. 'You can't state that kind of thing unreservedly. Y'see, for years up to just recently, our choir have been in the happy position of being almost completely ignored by the powers-that-be in the parish – just vaguely noticed as a collection of characters who seem to inhabit the choir stalls on Sundays, and who, back in the mists of time, were supposed to persuade the congregation to open their mouths during the singing of the hymns. Over the years the choir have sort of dissolved into the background and lived in our own independent world up there in the chancel. We sang whatever we liked and no one was interested enough to try to control us. It was great!' Olley sighed. 'And now the new tenor has dragged us into the limelight. Mind you, we're very pleased to have him. He's got a very powerful voice and we really *must* drown the vicar – his voice, that is, and this new man will help no end.'

'Well, there you are then,' I enthused, 'with a star like your new tenor, your choir will emerge from the shadows. You'll be popular. They'll be asking you to give recitals, take notice of what you say and do. There will be no more ignoring of the choir.'

Olley gazed at me pityingly and sighed in an exaggerated manner. 'That's just the trouble. Now, the vicar's warden and his plotters will grasp the opportunity to resurrect their grand plan for more trendy togetherness among the choir and the congregation. They're just living for the day when they can start ripping out the choir stalls and the pews and everyone can sit and sing, or not sing, together on nice, new orange plastic chairs.' Olley sighed gustily again. 'The choir will have to watch this situation very carefully,' he rumbled. 'Talk about "Fight the good fight".'

Some weeks after our meeting at the malfunctioning barrier, Olley and I met again at the same place and partook of the same sort of coffee with a lot of cream and grated chocolate on top . . .

It seemed that Olley's predictions about the great pew and choir-stall plot were coming to light rapidly. 'And how's the vicar coping?' I enquired. Olley considered for the briefest moment. 'Well, I suppose he's doing very much a "vicar thing". He's always been a pleasant kind of man who likes everything going along smoothly and no one rocking the boat. He's always been a good one at back clapping and hand pumping and congratulating people for doing nothing but turning up on time for church on Sundays.'

'And now?' I encouraged.

'Now,' growled Olley, prodding the coffee-table determinedly, 'because of the excitement over our new tenor, he's growing more and more convinced that the whole choir are so good that it's nothing short of a sin that we remain hidden up there in the choir stalls when we should be down in the nave among the congregation, letting the beauty of our singing flow over them, inspiring them to find the right hymn in their books and adventurously attempting to sing. (Yes, that's how bemused he's become since we fielded our star tenor!) Lately he's even managed to admire us and congratulate us at every service and he's stopped choir members in the street to confirm what a great pleasure it is for the congregation to be led by such beautiful singing of the psalms – such delicacy, such deep understanding of the words . . .'

'What? Your choir!' I gurgled.

Olley shrugged, 'Well admittedly the vicar's a complete musical moron, but he's making matters very dicey for the choir in view of the vicar's warden's campaign.'

'And,' I ventured, 'the choir wouldn't consider moving out of the choir stalls and scattering themselves among the congregation – to ease matters?'

Olley regarded me speechlessly for seconds. 'Look! Our choir are not into the vicar's warden's joyful togetherness thing – particularly sitting on plastic chairs. Our choir stalls are so comfortable anyway.' His manner became more serious. 'The trouble is going to get much worse soon – thanks, as usual, to the vicar's warden.' Olley stirred the remains of his sort of coffee quite violently and fixed me with an expression of mystified exasperation. 'I mean ter say, here we have a genuine middle-aged bachelor, for years only interested in cricket and steam engines and ordering people about at church, and suddenly last month he goes and gets snapped up by the new gym mistress at our school.'

'A whirlwind romance,' I enthused. 'How lovely!'

'Lovely?' Olley echoed. 'Lovely? This marriage could spell disaster for our choir! Y'see, this lady is a dedicated gardener – dedicated exclusively to her own ideas and raring to go to transform her new husband's tatty backyard and collapsed potting shed into a romantic rose garden.' I couldn't spot anything in the situation that should worry the choir. Olley went on thunderously. 'She's fallen in love with our *choir stalls*! The vicar's warden's campaign to do away with them is, of course, well known to her and she saw the stalls as the ideal furniture for her rose garden layout – as soon as the vicar's warden had cleared away the collapsed potting shed.'

'This new wife of the vicar's warden,' I said. 'Have you actually *met* her, *talked* with her about things? I wonder what she's really like, apart from being a yearner after discarded Victorian choir stalls and backyard rose gardens.' Olley smiled firmly. 'Well, Agatha's a sturdy no-nonsense lady with a determined expression and autocratic manner. She's one of those people who work at making themselves well known and liked – well known anyway – wherever they go. She doesn't exactly *mingle* with us locals, rather she sweeps among us at parish gatherings like the vicarage summer garden fête, and bring-and-buy lunches and the queue waiting to shake hands with the vicar after the service. She sweeps everywhere making sweeping statements. She's that sort of sweeping character.' Intrigued, I asked, 'So has she swept among the choir yet, seeing that she wants the choir stalls for her rose garden?'

But so intrigued had we become by the goings on at Olley's church – so immersed in the building up of a new choir sensation – that we had forgotten our coffee bar surroundings and our sort of coffee had gone cold and uninteresting. Olley consulted his watch and rose in one swift movement. 'Five minutes to my train – I'll email you,' he spluttered, and was gone.

Olley is a very bad typist and doesn't like sending emails. He says this modern craze for showering each other with emails is getting out of hand. He realized, of course, that as members of our modern, thrusting technologist society it is essential for all of us to keep the emails flowing in ever increasing floods – even if we've repeated messages and information to each other over and over again and often can't think of anything else to say but 'nothing has altered since yesterday'.

So dutifully Olley joined the mighty army of emailers and took up the drama of Agatha, the vicar's warden's new wife and the Victorian choir stalls. It was a long email in Olley's inimitable style that wandered off all over the place and only paused for breath at treble exclamation marks. I gathered vaguely that something quite unexpected had happened in Olley's parish which had twisted the drama in some way but I couldn't work out which way, as I'm sure Olley couldn't because only an hour after I'd received the email he was on the phone to me, eager to translate his email report.

The organist and choirmaster at Olley's church is an outwardly bland man, a pleasant middle-aged bachelor whom everyone in the parish smiles at vaguely when they happen to notice him in the village mini-market or, indeed, knock into him in the choir vestry. But, as Olley assures me now, there is a secret intriguing side to this retiring man of music which we in the church have seldom experienced, and now apparently the time for him to act positively had come.

Choral Evensong on Easter Sunday has always been a big occasion for the choir – when the congregation and the vicar do actually acknowledge the existence of the choir and put money in a collection box at the back of the church for the choir's summer outing fund. At the crowded gathering following the latest Easter Evensong, Agatha, the vicar's warden's striking new wife, was enjoying herself immensely, surrounded by her newfound admirers. Only after about an hour of non-stop flattery and when her feet in new, very high heeled shoes were killing her, she noticed the organist gazing at her, beaming vigorously. He came forward, almost bowing, and indicated a table for two just vacated. He wove his secret magic immediately. Keeping his voice low and intimate he told her, 'On Sunday, as the choir processes through the church and up into the choir stalls, singing the first hymn of the day, I am used to hearing the wavering warbles of the congregation with their heads drooping into their hymn books, causing, surely, the composer of the tune to turn in his grave.' The organist beamed at Agatha. 'But tonight, transforming the whole atmosphere, here you were, a presentation of vigorous enthusiasm, head held high, your hymn book raised before you, cheerful, inspiring, raising the whole tone . . . Dare I hope that you would consider joining our choir?'

Yes, of course, the lady *did* join the choir to assist the

wonderful organist to encourage the members to rise to unbelievable heights. And of course if the choir were going to be the showpiece of the church there was only one perfect setting for them, the choir stalls. They could not be left, decimated, among the congregation. Agatha had graciously agreed there would be no choir stalls in her new rose garden.

'One question,' I asked Olley. 'What is her voice *really* like? Pretty sensational I imagine, to cause all this excitement.' Olley seemed surprised at my question. 'We've no idea. She mimes quite well but we've never heard her sing. Our new tenor is pulling in the crowds. Everybody's happy!'